START A FAMILY FR

start a
FAMILY
FRIENDLY
BUSINESS

ANTONIA CHITTY
HELEN LINDOP

bookshaker

First Published in Great Britain 2010
by www.BookShaker.com

© Copyright Antonia Chitty and Helen Lindop

ACKNOWLEDGEMENTS

Without blogging I wouldn't have had the opportunity to write this book. So I want to thank everyone who inspired and taught me how to blog - the teams at Copyblogger and Problogger; Yaro Starak of Entrepreneur's Journey; Natalie Lue; David Meerman Scott, author of The New Rules of Marketing and PR and Caroline Middlebrook, author of The Blogger's Bible.

Thanks to my family for all your love and support – Rob, Aimee and Tom (I couldn't have done this without you), Mum and Dad, Grace, Jenni, Dave and Nan. Thanks to Sam, Helen and all of the girls at Mum's The Boss and to Bisola Orimalade and Sam Thewlis for being so supportive.

And a huge 'thank you' to Antonia Chitty for having faith in me as a newbie writer.

Helen Lindop

My thanks go to Sue Grindey who, many years ago, taught me that I could be something different: her faith in me saw me on the first of a number of career changes which left me so well placed when I started to run my own business. Without Suzy Greaves I'd never have had the confidence to take the first step to creating that business, so I am perpetually grateful to her. I'd like to thank Lindsey Columbell who introduced me to different ways to offer my services and expertise, and Karen Skidmore who is helping me to grow and develop my business.

Beyond that, I want to thank the fabulous women who are changing the way that mums can take part in the world of work, maximising flexibility and enterprise opportunities. Watch out for this generation of mums who are leading a revolution in the world of work, including Jane Hopkins, Nicky Chisholm, Roberta Jerram, Nadine Hill, Mel McGee, Sam Willoughby and Nikki Backshall. Keep at it!

I'd like to thank Helen for coming to me with this book idea and going through the writing process together. Special love and thanks to David, Daisy, Jay and Kit: the reasons I changed the way I work and my reasons for working.

Antonia Chitty

ABOUT THE AUTHORS

ANTONIA CHITTY has been working flexibly since having her daughter in 2002. She says, "On returning to work I felt like I was trying to do a full weeks work in part time hours, and spending all my money on childcare. Other people were looking after my daughter, and I was missing out on her growing up. I looked at the skills I had and how else I could apply them. A  session with a life coach really helped. I'd never thought of running my own business, but she opened my eyes to the fact that people would pay money for my skills."

Antonia explains, "I set up my own PR agency which focused on helping mums in business to do their own PR. That led to my first books, *A Guide to Promoting Your Business* and *Family Friendly Working*. I'm now working on my 14th book, and I love what I do."

Alongside this, Antonia is mum to Daisy, Jay and Kit. She says, "It's not always easy running your own business and being a mum at the same time. I couldn't do it without my partner, David. We both find there are never quite enough hours in the day to do everything, and you may find me typing frantically in the train on the way to a meeting, making the most of every moment I get. But I wouldn't change the way I work. I get to spend time with the kids, choose my own hours, and be there for events at school."

Antonia was awarded the 'Inspirational Business Mum of the Year' Award at the 2009 Mumpreneur Conference. She shares her business expertise with any mum who wants to set up a business through *The Mumpreneur Guide*.

HELEN LINDOP left her job as a trainer after having her first child as it involved frequent travel and it didn't suit part-time hours. She'd been a freelance before taking her last job, so she felt self-employment might give her the flexibility she wanted. She had an entrepreneurial streak and had assumed it would have to be put to one side until her children were  older, but now was her chance to use it. Helen started to research business ideas that could fit her and her new family and wrote about them on her blog *www.businessplusbaby.com*.

"I could have changed direction and found a different job, but seemed crazy to pay someone else a big chunk of my salary to care for my daughter when I wanted to be there with her myself" says Helen. "Once my son arrived, the cost of childcare for two children would have been so high that a nine-to-five job was no longer an option anyway. It's a good job that I was fascinated by small businesses – I didn't have much choice but to start one!"

Now mum to children aged one and two years, Helen has launched her new business, *www.helenlindop.com*, and will carry on blogging at *www.businessplusbaby.com* as her business develops.

"Starting a business as a mum to two young children is not easy, but it's giving me the freedom that employment simply couldn't. I want to be there for my children in their pre-school years and to be able to work around school hours and holidays too, so I see this business as an investment for the future" she says.

PRAISE

"If you are working full-time and missing being at home with your little one or you have a fabulous career but can't quite fathom how you are going to manage a family as well, then this book is great for opening up ideas. It is possible to juggle your life and a family as long as you have energy, drive and can find your niche in a Family-Friendly Business, so read on and good luck!"

Laura Tenison MBE, Founder & Managing Director, JoJo Maman Bébé

"I'm a huge advocate of mums who set up in business and who combine work and motherhood on their terms…and this book is a great starting point for anybody who's excited by this prospect. It's packed to the gunnels with good ideas and inspiration for harnessing the hidden mumpreneur inside!"

Wendy Shand, founder of www.totstotravel.co.uk

"This is a great resource for mums looking to go into business. Antonia and Helen have found all the best ways to get working for yourself that achieve the holy grail of minimising risk and maximising profit while letting you be a mum and manage some all-important me time too. I wish I'd had Business Ideas for Mums when I set out to be a mumpreneur - perhaps I wouldn't have made so many mistakes!"

Mosey Jones, author of 'The Mumpreneur Diaries'

"Here's a book brimming with straightforward, honest advice for the budding business mum. Any mum wondering where to start with business ideas and relevant information will find it in these pages. Antonia and Helen have done all the research so you don't have to! A great time saver."

Roberta Jerram, founder of GiantPotential.com & HWWBA Womanpreneur of the Year 2010

"What a fabulous book. Where was this 2 years ago when I was starting out? I love the clear and informative structure. The checklist of ones skills make it so much easier to work out which direction to go. The layout of the flexible working ideas provides you with all the answers and no questions! Just the way I like a book! Also taking into consideration your childcare arrangements even something I forget to consider now.
Joanne Dewberry, Dorset Business Mum of the Year, www.charliemoos.co.uk and www.networkingmummies.com

This is a great book if you find yourself in a position where your 'old' job no longer fits your new (with child) life. If you're open minded and ready to consider new avenues this book could be the catalyst to helping you find that holy grail - 'work/life balance'. The practical A-Z of flexible work ideas is excellent and even if you can't find one that fits you perfectly I'm sure it will throw up many more ideas that you can tailor your skills to. A great guide for mums ready to make a change!
Erica Douglas, www.littlemummy.com

"Loaded with useful and practical information, this is a book that will open up horizons. Combining motherhood and running your own business is not for the faint-hearted but this book clearly identifies a plethora of opportunities which are possible to run side-by-side. This is an absolute "must-read" for all mumpreneurs seeking inspiration and guidance on what to do in a no-nonsense, easy-to-read format."
Emma Wimhurst, founder of Diva Cosmetics

"A great guide to help any mum transition from 'thinker' to 'doer' when considering starting a business. The knowledge you will gain will help you to decide what kind of business might suit you and if indeed a business is the right solution for you. Knowledge is only power when you do something with it and the action plans at the end will help you to really make progress towards that flexible business you desire"
Mel McGee, author of 'Supermummy: The Ultimate Mumpreneur's Guide to Online Success', www.supermummy.com

"All you need to get started in business is an idea and a sprinkling of commitment. Any book that offers ideas will fire your imagination and help with the first step on what is sure to be an exciting journey!"

Emma Jones, founder of Enterprise Nation and author of 'Spare Room Start Up' and 'Working 5 to 9'

"I travel the British Isles running workshops and talking to mums who wish to set up in business for themselves. Whilst some have a really clear vision of what they want to do others have no idea where to start! Now I can point them to an in-depth, practical and fascinating book which clearly and honestly explores the myriad of possibilities. And, more importantly, helps to guide the reader towards the solution that would be the best fit for them. I loved this book. A truly excellent addition to business books for mumpreneurs."

Susan Odev, author of 'MumUltrapreneur', www.mum-ultrapreneur.com

CONTENTS

FOREWORD

Finding out I was pregnant for the first time, I travelled with much excitement to visit one of my brothers and tell him the good news. He was happy, gave me a big hug and said; "Well that's the end of your ambition, I suppose you will give up the business now?"

This comment was like a red rag to a bull; not only was I determined to *never* lose my commercial drive and passion for the brand, but I desperately wanted a family and to be a hands-on mum. The year after my son was born JoJo nearly doubled turnover and I breastfed Ben till he was 9 months old. I was there for my children *and* there for the company which is not an easy choice and one which meant I hardly got any sleep and had to become a very low maintenance girl. But I would not have had it any other way.

If you are working full-time and missing being at home with your little one or you have a fabulous career but can't quite fathom how you are going to manage a family as well, then this book is great for opening up ideas. It is possible to juggle your life and a family as long as you have energy, drive and can find your niche in a Family-Friendly Business, so read on and good luck!

Laura Tenison MBE
Founder & Managing Director
JoJo Maman Bébé

INTRODUCTION

IF YOU'VE BOUGHT THIS BOOK BECAUSE YOU ARE LOOKING FOR FLEXIBLE AND FAMILY FRIENDLY WORK, YOU'RE IN THE RIGHT PLACE!

We've brought together the best ideas from our sites, *www.familyfriendlyworking.co.uk* and *www.businessplusbaby.com* and added in loads more ideas and resources to help you find **work** that is right for you and will fit with your **family**.

We've both got experience of being where you are now. We've found that the work we did before having children just didn't fit, and we know how hard it can be to find the right **opportunity**. And we're not alone. Three quarters (76%) of mothers who are not currently working for themselves would do so if they had the chance. And nearly half of all British mums (47%) are actually considering starting their own business, but do not know where to start. *

So, we've done some of the hard work for you. We list **129 top ideas for businesses and flexible work**, and outline the pros and cons of 23 of them so you can pick the one that appeals to you.

Each of the **23 business idea pages** also contains further resources so you know where to go next, plus additional **bonus business ideas** to really get you thinking about ALL the opportunities there are out there.

Read on to get the inside take on 129 great business ideas. Our advice will give you a head start and help you create the flexible work-life balance that you want.

Antonia Chitty
Family Friendly Working
www.familyfriendlyworking.co.uk

Helen Lindop
Business Plus Baby
www.businessplusbaby.com

---

* Survey of 1000 mothers with children under the age of 18 in the UK in March 2010 by Redshift Research and social network MumsLikeYou for Phoenix Trading.

ALL ABOUT YOU

Before you start looking through the business ideas, take some time to think about YOU. If you know your skills, are clear about the time you have available and know what you enjoy doing you're more likely to pick an idea that works well for you and your family.

What are you good at?

Without thinking for too long, write down five things that you think you are good at. Just pop down the first things that come to mind.

Now, ask someone who knows you well to tell you five things that they think you are good at.

Look at these lists of your **strengths**. Understanding your strengths will help you when you are looking at the ideas in this book.

When can you work?

Fill in the hours you have available for work: remember that you need time with your partner and time to relax too.

Here's an example:

	SUNDAY	MONDAY	TUESDAY	WEDNESDAY	THURSDAY	FRIDAY	SATURDAY
MORNING			10-12 while son is at nursery		10-12 while son is at nursery		
AFTERNOON							
EVENEING	7-9	7-9	7-9	7-9			

Now fill in your own:

	SUNDAY	MONDAY	TUESDAY	WEDNESDAY	THURSDAY	FRIDAY	SATURDAY
MORNING							
AFTERNOON							
EVENEING							

What do you enjoy?

You are far more likely to make a success of a business or job if you also enjoy it. Quickly, write down five things that you enjoy doing.

What do these things have in common? What does it show you about yourself? Do you like doing things with others or by yourself? Do you enjoy detailed tasks or thinking about the broad picture? Think about what you'd like to spend your time doing and bear this in mind when working through this book and considering the various ideas for flexible work.

What do you want from a business?

Do you want a part-time income only until your children all reach school age? Or a business that can grow and take on employees, franchisees or hire freelances?

And for how long do you want to run this business? Is it something that you see as a short term option before going back to employment, or is it going to carry you through to retirement, or is it a business that you will grow to sell on in five or ten years time?

14 TIPS FOR MUMPRENEUR SUCCESS

1. List your priorities such as earning money, or finding work that lets you stay home with your children. Then, write down your skills, and ask others what they think you're good at.
2. Think about the hours you can devote to work. Be realistic if you plan to work around the kids, as children may not understand "mummy's working". Write down your work hours, whether they are 12-2 each day during nap time, 9.30-11.30 to fit with nursery, 7-9 in the evenings or a combination on different days.
3. Consider what sort of business will fit your needs. If you plan to offer a service, it may be limited to the hours you have available unless you take on others to help you. If you want to offer a product, is it something handmade you will offer on a small scale, or do you want a product that you can scale up?
4. Research the market for your business. Will people buy your product or service? Is it unique enough to be appealing? Look at your competition and work out how your business could be different or better.
5. Develop a vision for your life and your business. The clearer your vision, the easier it will be to work out the steps you need to take to achieve it.
6. Work out your exit strategy. When might you want to move on from this business? How could you sell it? Work this out early on as otherwise it can be very difficult when you find your needs have changed and the business no longer fits.
7. Prepare a business plan. Set out aims and objectives, and the steps you need to take to achieve your goals. Pop into a local Enterprise Agency for advice. See if they offer a free start up course, a great way to get your business plan going.

8. Register as self employed. You have 3 months to let the Inland Revenue know you have started a business, or you could end up with a £100 fine.

9. Work out how you will promote and market your business. Have a promotion planning session where you investigate advertising, marketing, PR and events. Note on a wall calendar what activities you will do each month to promote the business. Spend 15 minutes each day on promotion.

10. Promote your business online. Start a Twitter account in the name of your business, create a blog and a Facebook fan page. To make things easier use Twitterfeed or Friendfeed to link your different networking sites together.

11. Keep good records. It is easier to note down every item of expenditure from the start than to have to deal with a pile of receipts when your tax return is due in. You can claim many of your business costs against tax too. The Inland Revenue can send an advisor to your house who can talk you through what you can claim.

12. Make the most of every customer. From day one, start a customer database so you can send out regular newsletter and exclusive subscriber offers. It is easier to get existing customers to buy again than to find new ones.

13. Get some great support. Go back to your list of skills and add in areas that you struggle with. Allow in your business plan for help: you could find a bookkeeper, or get someone to help with PR, marketing, packing and post office runs or admin. This can allow your business to grow and develop and mean you spend your time most effectively.

14. Watch out for your work-life balance. Business can easily take over. Have a finish time each day, put your work away, and make some time to relax.

If you're serious about starting a business, check out *www.themumpreneurguide.co.uk* for a book specially designed for mums who want to start a family friendly business. It covers issues from business planning to childcare, finances to setting aside time for you. It is the best way to give your new business a head start.

23 TIPS FOR WORKING AROUND A FAMILY

WORKING WHEN YOU HAVE A FAMILY IS A SKILL THAT IT TAKES TIME TO LEARN. COMPARED TO WHEN IT WAS JUST YOU THERE ARE DIFFERENT NEEDS TO JUGGLE. CHILDCARE IS EXPENSIVE AND YOU MAY PREFER TO LOOK AFTER YOUR CHILDREN YOURSELF. READ OUR TIPS BASED ON OUR OWN EXPERIENCES AND ON THOSE OF OTHER FAMILIES...

If you have under-fives with you as you work

Many mums avoid working with toddlers underfoot as they feel they are not being fair to their business or their children. Others decide that they are working in a flexible way just BECAUSE they want to be with the children at home, and accept the limitations that this presents. It's certainly not an easy option and you are bound to have many distractions as the children might not understand that "mummy needs to work now". Here are some tips:

- ✓ Allocate regular periods of time to focus one-hundred percent on the children. Don't have one eye on your inbox as you're playing with toy cars, for example.

- ✓ Before you start work, give your children an activity to do. Perhaps they could sit beside you and draw pictures as you work?

- ✓ There are some tasks you can do in a quick ten-minute slot here and there, such as checking email, Facebook or Twitter. Other tasks that require more concentration may need be left until your children are not around.

- ✓ Rather than trying to get bits and pieces of work done throughout the day, you could focus on getting the children to bed promptly every evening so you can get on with your work in peace.

- ✓ Be realistic about what you can achieve in the time you have.

Childcare options

For many mums, the main reason for starting a business is to be able to spend more time with their families. But it's very hard to run a business as mum to under-fives with no childcare at all. Fortunately, if you run a flexible business you can be more flexible with your childcare choices than most employees:

✓ You can choose to do a proportion of your work in the evening when the children are in bed, or some during the day if they nap. This cuts down on the number of childcare hours you need and therefore the cost. You also get to spend more time with your children when they are awake than you would if you worked nine-to-five.

✓ Because you can break up your working day into an hour here and an hour there, two and a half hour preschool sessions could be more practical than they might for an employee. You do need to be organised to work in such a fragmented way, though. Make a plan for your business and list the tasks you need to do each week and month. That way you can get straight to work when you do have a chance.

✓ Your children could be in your home, but supervised by someone else. Maybe you could get a teenage neighbour to entertain your children for a couple of hours after school? A babysitter like this is invaluable and may be available to help with school holidays or sick days if needed.

✓ Could you arrange to 'swap' children with another mum for a morning a week? She doesn't have to be a business mum: every mum enjoys a little me-time.

In the school holidays

The school holidays can be a headache for mums in business. Some accept that they aren't going to be doing much work and reduce their workload down to a minimum. Other options include:

✓ The childcare options used by other working parents. Look into local holiday clubs and ask grandparents or uncles and aunties if they could help for a day each week or for an overnight stay.

✓ Arrange child swaps and playdates with other families: if your children have friends over they may all disappear off and play, and if not you'll always know that they will be out all day the following week.

✓ If it's appropriate and your children are willing, you could involve them in your business. Perhaps they could help you run a stand at a craft fair or pack some orders ready for posting. This could be a good lesson in entrepreneurship!

✓ Create rotas for making lunch if your children are old enough as this can save you time and give them the chance to get creative in the kitchen and learn important life skills. A little light supervision can stop the kitchen looking like a disaster zone when they have finished.

✓ If you do work during the school holidays, try to take regular time off (maybe a day a week) to do some activities with your children.

✓ A mix of these methods works well for most mums: schedule in some work days when you have someone to help with the kids or when you simply let them follow their natural inclination to sleep in and watch TV in their pyjamas all morning. Have some days out where you are 100% on holiday yourself: even if you take a picnic to the park just switch off your phone and let the business look after itself for a few hours.

✓ Finally, lower your standards. Accept that you can't do everything over the holidays. Prioritise time with the kids, do what you need to keep the business going, and accept that the house is going to be more messy than usual.

Don't forget

❑ Watch out for your work-life balance. Business can easily take over. Have a finish time each day, put your work away, and make some time to relax.

❑ Remember what's important to you. If you are running your business so you can be there for the children, don't let it take over all your time together.

❑ Don't stress about the state of your house. Something will have to give and it will probably be the housework. Being able to ignore a pile of laundry and get on with your work is an asset if you run a business from home!

❑ Be realistic about the hours you can devote to working.

❑ Allow enough time to spend with your partner or your relationship could suffer.

❑ Your time is precious, so spend it on the things you are good at or enjoy doing. Hate bookkeeping? Get a bookkeeper! Or find another business mum and work on a project together and work to your strengths.

❑ And book in 'me-time' every week so you can have a long bath, a coffee with a friend, or time to paint your toenails!

THE A-Z OF FLEXIBLE WORK IDEAS

ANTENATAL TEACHER

What is it?

An antenatal teacher helps pregnant women prepare for birth using techniques like hypnotherapy, visualisation, relaxation, exercise or yoga.

Tell me more...

A complementary therapist might specialise in working with mums-to-be and use therapies such as reflexology, Reiki and massage to do the same.

These techniques may also be used to help women recover after the birth, to adjust to motherhood or get back into shape after having a baby.

What are the benefits?

- If you are passionate about pregnancy and birth this is a perfect opportunity to work with women at a fascinating time in their lives.
- As mothers and mothers-to-be, your clients will usually be happy for you to work around your family.
- Working hours are flexible and will often be in the evening or at weekends to fit in with your clients work and family commitments.

Things to consider...

Your clients will only need your services for a period of a few months, so you'll need to think of ways of catching them early on in their pregnancies. Unless you have lots of clients who go on to have big families, you won't get much repeat custom either! But you could encourage clients to recommend you to their pregnant friends, perhaps by giving them discount vouchers.

It's a good idea to make sure your website appears near the top of the search results in search engines. For example, if you're a maternity reflexologist in Coventry, aim to be top of the list when someone types 'maternity reflexology Coventry' into Google. Potential clients will then find you if they have decided they want your service but haven't yet found a local teacher or therapist.

You can improve your cash-flow by selling courses, rather than individual sessions. It means that you know you have covered your costs (such as room hire) at the start of a course rather than having to worry about it before every session.

You could offer several different therapies or courses. This might mean being a therapist with a pregnancy specialism (a reflexologist who also does maternity reflexology) or a pregnancy/birth specialist who offers several courses or therapies (e.g. hypnotherapy and reiki).

Further information

- Training to be an antenatal teacher, breastfeeding counsellor or postnatal leader with the National Childbirth Trust - *www.nct.org.uk/newdirections*
- Teacher training for the Active Birth method - *activebirthcentre.com*
- Teacher training for Hypnobirthing - *www.hypnobirthing.co.uk*
- Training for reflexologists who want to specialise in maternity reflexology - *www.maternity-reflexology.com*
- Training to teach yoga in pregnancy – *www.birthlight.com*

You might also like

- ❑ Independent midwife
- ❑ Doula
- ❑ Yoga teacher

Other Business Ideas Beginning with A

- ❑ Avon representative
- ❑ Acupuncturist
- ❑ Aromatherapist

BOOKKEEPER

What is it?

A bookkeeper keeps detailed records of a business' financial transactions.

Tell me more...

By starting a book keeping business, you might be working for small businesses that don't need their own full time bookkeeper or perhaps need an extra bookkeeper at a busy time.

You may have previous experience of similar work and decide to go freelance or you could change careers completely and retrain as a bookkeeper.

What are the benefits?

- You can often work from home, although some clients might expect you to work from their office. If you want to work from home only, make sure your potential client is aware of this before they hire you.

- You can take on as many or as few clients as you want, giving you control over the number of hours you work.

- You can work flexible hours to fit in around a family.

Things to consider...

You need to be well organised, methodical person who enjoys getting numbers to add up accurately.

Clients will need to trust you before they let you work on their books. This is one reason why marketing methods where you build a relationship with potential clients are likely to work better than, say, leaflet drops and print advertising.

Attending business networking events would be a good place to start building these business relationships. You could also answer questions in an online forum, so when people realise they're struggling with their books, they call you. (Always check the rules of the forum first, though.)

Word of mouth referrals can be very effective - make sure all your friends, family and neighbours know about your service so you get a mention whenever anyone asks them "do you know a good bookkeeper?"

Accountants often outsource work to bookkeepers, so this could be a good way to get work. As with other types of client, try getting to know local accountants rather than just writing to them.

You will need to register with HMRC for Money Laundering Regulations (unless you are a member of a designated professional body).

See *www.hmrc.gov.uk/mlr/getstarted/register/who.htm* for more information.

Although a bookkeeping business is often considered cheap to start, you'll need to pay for accounting software, professional indemnity insurance, possibly membership of a professional body (such as ICB) and registration for money laundering. Don't forget to take these costs into account when deciding what to charge your clients.

You could progress to more advanced courses in bookkeeping and accounts. This could allow you to expand your business or to get employment in this field when your children are older.

Further information

Professional organisations (websites also include details of approved training providers):

- Institute of Certified Bookkeepers - *www.bookkeepers.org.uk*

- Association of Accounting Technicians - *www.aat.org.uk*

- IAB - *www.iab.org.uk*

- National Extension College offers bookkeeping courses by distance learning - *www.nec.ac.uk*

You Might Also Like
- ❏ Virtual Assistant

Other Business Ideas Beginning with 'B'
- ❏ Ballet teacher
- ❏ Balloon Artist
- ❏ Beauty therapist
- ❏ Bettaware agent
- ❏ Blogger
- ❏ Bookkeeper
- ❏ Bricks and mortar shop
- ❏ Building flatpack furniture
- ❏ Business coach

CHILDREN'S PARTY ENTERTAINER

What is it?

Entertaining children at birthday parties and other events.

Tell me more...

Many parents want to give their children a memorable birthday party but can't face entertaining a crowd of excitable children themselves. If you do love entertaining children, a children's party business could be right up your street.

Here are some ideas...

- Being a clown
- Running party games
- Face painting
- Art and craft parties
- Cooking parties
- Music parties. You sing, play an instrument and maybe bring instruments for the children too.
- Soft play parties. You provide the equipment to the parents' venue of choice such as their garden or a hired community centre.
- Pampering and beauty parties
- Or a whole-party package where you provide food, plates, cups, party bags, entertainment and clear up afterwards.

You can tailor your service to fit your previous experience, interests or to enhance a business you already run. For example a beauty therapist could run pampering parties or someone already running a pre-school class might branch out into art and craft parties. Mums who run music and activity classes for pre-schoolers often run parties at weekends as a way to boost their business income at a time when their partner can look after the kids.

What are the benefits?

If you love working with children this could be great fun.

The work is likely to be at the weekend so if you have a partner who works Monday to Friday, you could share the childcare between you and not have to pay for a childminder or nursery.

By putting your website and contact details on your party invitations and in party bags, you can cheaply and easily market your services to other children and parents.

Start up costs are usually low compared to some businesses. You can try a few parties to see if you enjoy it and to test the market without investing too much time or money.

You could branch out: a face painter or clown could be hired for weddings to keep children entertained during the speeches.

Things to consider...

You must be reliable. If you take a booking and then don't show up, you're ruining a child's birthday party. This is not only disappointing for the children, it's bad for your business. You need to be sure that you're committed to running the parties you have booked. Also, what will you do if you, or your own children, are ill? It could be worth making contact with other mums in the same line of work so you can cover for each other.

If you're doing a job you love and that's based around having fun, it's easy to short-change yourself because it seems mean to ask for much money. Remember you have a talent, you're providing a service that people want and you're entitled to be paid what you're worth.

If you take into account travel costs, good quality equipment, party bags, any future training you might want to do, food (if you're providing it), set up and clearing-away time and insurance, the fee you need to charge to make a living may seem quite high. It's easy to start off by saying "I'll charge £2 per child because that's reasonable" only to find that this doesn't even cover your costs, let alone pay you a wage. It's best to avoid this by setting a realistic fee from the start.

Parents will be trusting you with their children - if you're too cheap, that might suggest that you're not properly qualified, experienced or reliable. Look into getting a CRB (Criminal Records Bureau) check or Disclosure Scotland check. This is not compulsory at time of writing but can reassure parents who are considering booking you. See the section on Tutoring for more on CRB checks.

Look carefully at how you charge. If you charge per child and only three show up, you'll be out of pocket. If you charge per hour or per party then the onus is on the parent to get enough children to make it worthwhile. You could have a minimum number to book, or you could charge a flat fee for the first (say) ten children then a price per child above that number.

Don't forget to get adequate insurance. Whether you're painting faces or encouraging children to run around like wild things, the potential for mishaps is high!

Do you want to work weekends? Working weekends means that you will be missing time with your partner and your own children - how much does this bother you?

Further information

- *www.netmums.com* has a thread on its forum for children's party entertainers and organisers.

- *www.bemybearparties.co.uk* has entertainers who run bear-making parties - could you become a party entertainer for them or use this as inspiration for your own party theme?

- *www.uk-entertainers.co.uk* will give you some ideas of what other entertainers do and sometimes what they charge.

- *www.splatcooking.net* runs children's cooking parties and offer franchises.

You might also like

- ❑ Childminder
- ❑ Under-fives group leader

Other Business Ideas Beginning with 'C'

- ❑ Candle maker
- ❑ Car cleaning and repair franchisee
- ❑ Card maker
- ❑ Childminder
- ❑ Chocolate maker
- ❑ Classroom assistant
- ❑ Cleaner
- ❑ Coach
- ❑ Community magazine editor
- ❑ Complementary therapist
- ❑ Cook and caterer
- ❑ Copywriter
- ❑ Cosmetics maker
- ❑ Counsellor
- ❑ Crochet
- ❑ CV writer

DROP SHIPPING

What is it?

If you want to run an online retail business but don't already have a product, drop shipping might work for you.

Drop shipping means that you generate orders and send them through to a supplier who delivers them directly to a customer. You do not need to invest in and hold stock, which reduces your start up costs.

Tell me more...

Some businesses hold some stock but use drop shipping as a way to deal with bulky or expensive items that they don't have space to store or funds to invest in.

You can drop ship a wide range of products including:

- Football kit
- Perfume and beauty products
- Baby gear, from cloth nappies to prams

What are the benefits?

The main plus points of drop shipping are that you cut out the need to:

- invest in stock
- find somewhere to store it
- deal with packing products up
- take your orders to the post office

If you have an existing business and use drop shipping for a few expensive and bulky items it can allow you to increase your range at little cost.

Things to consider...

Many drop shipping companies ask for an initial investment from you. This can be as little as £20-£30, or may be higher and include your own website to sell from.

With drop shipping you will get a percentage of the sale price, but you will earn less than if you had bought the stock wholesale. That's because you are leaving someone else to carry the burden of holding stock, packing and dispatching it. You may only earn a few pounds per item, so you can need to sell quite a lot of products to make a good income.

If you go for the approach of only selling items from one drop shipper and there are plenty of other people doing the same, it can be hard to find customers. Just having a site full of products does not mean people will buy: you need to do just as much work as any other business owner to drive traffic to the site.

Further information

There are enterprises that offer to set you up in a drop shipping business, and some even offer to set you up with a website of your own. Find drop shippers at:

- The Wholesaler UK - *www.thewholesaler.co.uk/trade/distributor/Dropshippers_ and_dropshipping_directory*

- ATS Distribution - *www.atsdistribution.co.uk/Dropship.aspx*

- Puckator: *www.puckator.co.uk*

- The Select - *www.theselect.co.uk/catalogue/browse.php?product_Categ ory_ID=180*

- *www.netmums.com* has a thread on its 'Working for Yourself' forum for drop shippers.

You might also like

- ❑ eBay
- ❑ Online store
- ❑ Party plan and direct selling

Other Business Ideas Beginning with 'D'

- ❑ Dating service
- ❑ Declutterer
- ❑ Decorator
- ❑ Delivery and van based franchisee
- ❑ Direct sales – see party plan
- ❑ Distributor
- ❑ Dog walking and pet sitting
- ❑ Doula

EBAY

What is it?

Making an income from selling on auction website eBay.

Tell me more...

eBay is a good choice if you want to start an online store but aren't ready for the work involved in running and promoting your own website. Many mums start off their online store by selling their own unwanted items on eBay, then move on to their own website when they feel ready.

What are the benefits?

- You can work at any time of the day or night - although you'll need to respond to customers promptly.
- You can spend as much or as little time on it as you want.
- It's cheap and quick to start up compared with setting up your own online shop.

Things to consider...

Items on eBay are usually at a low price - this is because you are competing in a marketplace with thousands of sellers, many of whom aren't looking to make much of a profit. As well as people looking to clear their lofts, you're competing with shop owners who are shifting excess stock and ends of lines. This allows them to keep their prices at a reasonable level on their own websites or in their high street shops. You'll need to choose your product carefully if you're going to make an income rather than just a few pounds here and there.

Look for items you can get hold of cheaply and easily but that others probably can't. Do you have a factory shop near you? Do you have an eye for good quality items at car boot sales? Do you have an interest in something vintage? You could try selling a few different types of items and see which bring in the best profit.

If you're emptying your loft, then you probably don't need to declare the income you make from this to HMRC (although check this out if you're in any doubt). But if you're making an income from selling on eBay you'll need to register as self employed.

Further information
- Register as self employed at *www.hmrc.gov.uk*

How to sell on eBay:
- Look for the guides on how to sell and the fees charged at *www.ebay.com*
- Mums Club has a useful guide to selling on eBay: *www.mumsclub.co.uk/html/selling_on_ebay.html*

Alternatives to eBay for crafts and handmade items:
- *www.etsy.com*
- *www.dawanda.co.uk*
- *www.folksy.com*
- *www.misi.co.uk*

Amazon:
- Click the 'selling' links on the homepage at *www.amazon.co.uk*

Other auction sites (although these have many fewer visitors than the mighty eBay):
- *uk.ebid.net*
- *www.cqout.com*
- *www.specialistauctions.com*

You might also like
- ❑ Drop shipping
- ❑ Online store
- ❑ Party planner
- ❑ Stall Holder

Other Business Ideas Beginning with 'E'
- ❑ Embroidery
- ❑ Estate agent and property services franchisee
- ❑ Event management

FRANCHISING

What is it?

If you want a tried and tested business idea and have some money to invest, buying a franchise can give you a business of your own but with training and support from head office.

Tell me more...

A franchise gives you the right to run a business, usually in a certain area. You will be supported with logos and promotional material, and given guidance on procedures. You may be given equipment as part of the start up package.

You can buy a business franchise for an enormous range of enterprises including:

- Delivery services
- Photo development
- Dating services
- Clothing
- Fast food outlets
- Education and training

What are the benefits?

If you buy a franchise your investment will get you:

- Support
- Training
- Tried and tested procedures and systems
- The benefit of a recognised brand
- Advertising, marketing and PR
- In house accounts support
- Discounts and savings on purchases of new materials, insurance etc.

Things to consider...

When you are looking into getting a franchise, check out the franchises operating in neighbouring areas. Ask to visit and talk to the owners. Find out from them what the key factors are in their success and what are the main problems they have to overcome. Think about whether you could replicate their success in your area.

Remember that some franchise opportunities give you exclusive rights to an area but others don't: always check what you are getting.

Find out about the initial fee, and then any ongoing fees that you need to pay to the franchisor for business support. You may need to pay a percentage of turnover (note – not profit) or an annual licence fee. The royalty fee is also often used for ongoing training of the franchisee and their staff. There may be other fees associated with a franchise, such as advertising along with the requirement to purchase specialised equipment and all supplies from the franchisor.

Take advice from a solicitor and accountant before signing up for any franchise.

Further information

There is an enormous amount of information out there for you if you are thinking of buying a franchise, but remember that most of it is created by the people who want to sell their opportunity to you.

You can visit franchise exhibitions, subscribe to franchise magazines and check out sites that list franchises. Here are a few resources to help you start researching the different opportunities:

- British Franchise Association - *www.thebfa.org* - 01491 578050
- Franchise Alliance - *www.myfranchise.net* - 0845 838 3070
- Franchise Direct - *www.franchisedirect.co.uk* – 353 1 865 6370 (Ireland)
- The UK Franchise Directory - *www.theukfranchisedirectory.net* - 01603 620 301

- Which Franchise - *www.whichfranchise.com*
  - 0141 204 0050
- Franchise Gator - *www.franchisegator.co.uk*
  - 0845 363 7165
- Create - *www.createproject.org.uk* - impartial advice on franchising, direct selling, licensing and distribution
- Find a list of Franchise opportunities on Family Friendly Working - *www.familyfriendlyworking.co.uk*

You might also like

- ❑ Drop shipping
- ❑ Online store
- ❑ Party planning and direct sales

Other Business Ideas Beginning with 'F'

- ❑ Floristry
- ❑ Forum host
- ❑ Financial services franchisee
- ❑ Fitness

GRAPHIC DESIGNER

What is it?

As a Graphic Designer, you will find yourself creating artwork using print, electronic and film media. Your work will become company logos, leaflets, flyers and other promotional materials, and is likely to be used online too. You may develop a specialism, working with advertising or in publishing on the overall layout and design of magazines, newspapers, journals, corporate reports and other publications

Tell me more...

To train as a Graphic Designer you will find computer skills essential. Artistic ability is what will set you apart from the competition. Win clients by understanding their brief and coming up with creative and innovative proposals.

What are the benefits?

- This works well for mums as you can do much of your work as a graphic designer at home on your computer
- You can choose how many hours you work
- You can work weekends and evenings

Things to consider...

Are you good at learning to use different computer programmes. Graphic designers typically use software such as:

- Adobe® FrameMaker®
- Adobe® Acrobat®
- Adobe® Photoshop®
- Adobe® Indesign®
- Adobe® Illustrator®

Basic knowledge of MS Office is useful and you'll need access to that or something similar as many clients supply files as word docs or spreadsheets. Open Office is a free alternative.

Work out which programmes you'll need to invest in to get started. Consider whether your home computer is up to the job: a large screen and ability to handle large files makes the job of a graphic designer much easier.

Many designers use Macs rather than PCs. They are generally more compatible with printing technology. On the downside, Macs are more expensive.

You also need to consider your skills with drawing, colours and lettering, plus have some mathematical ability and learn about printing techniques.

Some graphic designers have developed their skills themselves, but most have come through a bachelor's degree in art or design and taken further training. There are lots of courses leading to qualifications in design at universities and art colleges throughout the UK. Because there are numerous courses, this is a competitive area to break into.

Can you work to tight deadlines? Clients often need work done to fit in with print and other business deadlines so you'll need to be able to meet these. This can mean working late in the evenings or calling in extra help looking after the family.

Are you able to juggle? You are likely to have several clients' projects to work on at once with different deadlines for each. You may need to be your own IT department and cope with all the other sides of the business too.

As more and more businesses develop an online presence opportunities for graphic designers will continue to grow. A website of your own is an essential to showcase your work and attract new clients. As with any small business you will need to develop the skills to market yourself and learn about how much to charge to ensure that you make a decent living.

If you are starting from scratch you may need to take small jobs for other small businesses to build up a portfolio: if you have worked as a graphic designer before having children but are beginning as a freelancer call up former colleagues and ask for work as they will know and appreciate your skills already.

Remember, like all businesses offering professional services, to get professional indemnity insurance.

Further information

- The Chartered Society of Designers - *www.csd.org.uk*
- The Design Business Association - *www.dba.org.uk*
- The Design Council - *www.designcouncil.org.uk*
- Your Creative Future - *www.yourcreativefuture.org*
- UK Graphic Designers Directory - *www.ukgraphicdesigner.co.uk*

Read:

- *Design Week*, Centaur Communications
- *Creative Review*, Centaur Communications

You might also like

- ❑ Advertising creative copywriter
- ❑ Artist
- ❑ Illustrator
- ❑ Marketing
- ❑ Photographer
- ❑ Website designer

Other Business Ideas Beginning with 'G'

- ❑ Gardener
- ❑ Glass painting
- ❑ Greeting card distribution
- ❑ Gym Class Leader

HOLISTIC/COMPLEMENTARY THERAPIST

What is it?

A holistic therapist offers one or more of a range of therapies to help people look after their mind, body and spirit.

Tell me more...

Many mums have always wanted to work in the complementary health field, so take opportunity to retrain as therapists when they have children. There is a huge range of therapies to choose from, including:

- Herbalism, homeopathy, aromatherapy, flower remedies, Oriental herbal medicine
- Reiki, energy healing, spiritual healing, crystal therapy.
- Hypnotherapy, counselling, psychotherapy, neuro linguistic programming (NLP)
- Indian head massage, sports massage, aromatherapy massage
- Chiropractic, osteopathy
- Reflexology, hopi ear candles, stone therapy, Alexander Technique
- And many more!

What are the benefits?

- You can choose how many hours you work
- You can work weekends and evenings
- This could be the chance to do the type of work you've always wanted to do

Things to consider...

You can work from home, in other people's homes or rent a room from a clinic, natural therapy centre or hairdressing salon.

If you work from a clinic, centre or salon, you will almost certainly have to do some, if not all, of your own marketing.

Marketing methods that work well for this type of business are:

- Taster sessions (perhaps as part of a pampering evening) often run as fundraisers for schools.
- A leaflet campaign backed up by a website which gives people further info - leaflets could go through local people's doors, be left in business centre receptions, GP surgeries, libraries, railway stations, gyms or handed out to everyone you know.
- Local websites such as *www.gumtree.com*
- Postcards in local shop windows.
- Get an article in a local newspaper.
- Use your car - put a sign in the back window or magnetic adverts on the doors (check out *www.vistaprint.co.uk*).

This section covers a huge range of therapies, so the time and effort needed to get qualified varies from part time weekend training to a five year degree course. The first place to look for training would be your local further education college or *www.naturaltherapypages.co.uk*.

You can do some training by distance learning, although you'll need to weigh up how effective this is for learning 'hands on' skills. You can study subjects such as anatomy and physiology successfully, though.

Further information

- *www.healthypages.co.uk* is a mine of useful information and a place to advertise your services
- *www.itecworld.co.uk* is the exam board for beauty and complementary therapies as well as yoga, Pilates etc.

You might also like

❑ Sports Therapist
❑ Beauty Therapist
❑ Yoga, Tai Chi, Meditation or Pilates Teacher

Other Business Ideas Beginning with 'H'

❑ Hairdresser
❑ House cleaning
❑ House finding
❑ Human resources

INVENTOR
(OF A NEW PRODUCT)

What is it?

Many mums find that being at home with a new baby sparks a creative streak. Some find new solutions to baby related problems while others take advantage of time spent feeding to dream up an invention that has nothing to do with babies. So being an inventor involves designing or creating a new kind of product or invention that you can see an unfulfilled demand for in the marketplace.

Tell me more...

Coming up with the initial idea for an innovative product is simply the first step on a very long route to get an invention from concept to market. Cally Robson of *www.shesingenious.org* says, "With the spread of the Internet it's never been easier to develop and commercialize an innovative product or invention yourself. It's already big in the US, with many women choosing this as a way to get into business. In the UK too, it's easy to come up with an idea you can research online, check out the Intellectual Property you can register to protect it, design it yourself or find a designer to make a prototype for you, source suppliers and manufacturers, and either sell it yourself via the Web, or to retailers and distributors, or license the concept to industry players who will manufacture and market it, giving you a percentage of the sales."

What are the benefits?

Inventing your own product means that you have something totally unique – you hope – with the potential for enormous profits. On the downside, though, it takes persistence to turn your idea onto a product that people can buy. Cally Robson explains, "If you research and develop your product right:

- You can be your own boss and work flexibly.

- Your business will be scalable and profitable because you can sell more products without putting in a proportionate amount of your time. Some products that catch on can turn over millions of pounds a year such as Mandy Haberman's Anyway Up Cup or Natalie Ellis's Road Refresher, a non-spill pet bowl.

- If you get the knack for creating licensable products, you sit back and watch the royalties roll in while someone else does the manufacturing and marketing.

- Your product, and the intellectual property in it, becomes an asset that has a value. This means you can sell your business when you want out. Sometimes for a few million pounds.

- It's incredibly satisfying to design or invent something useful.

- The development journey is complex, but very rewarding if you take it step by step, getting the right support and advice along the way."

Things to consider...

Cally Robson explains, "The toughest part is having a really useful idea that hasn't been done before, AND that will make a profit after all the development and manufacturing costs are counted in.

"Funding is rarely available to help solo inventors. The prototyping and patenting can be costly, anything from £3000 to £300,000. So it's not something to get into if you have no money to invest.

"Returns aren't usually quick. Not only because the development and prototyping time takes longer than most people expect: think a year to 18 months for a designed product, 3 to 8 years for a patented one. But getting it into the market usually takes longer because people don't plan for this upfront."

If you have created something that is new and unique you will need to look at registering or patenting the design. Registering a design can be done relatively quickly and will cost less than a few hundred pounds. Patenting is a much longer process.

If you have designed something, you have 12 months from making the product public to register the design with the UK Intellectual Property Office. Look through catalogues, search on the internet, and check existing registered designs to make sure your design is new and unique. You then need to fill in forms from the UKIPO website to register. It costs around £60 and will protect your design for up to 25 years, renewable every five years.

A patent protects the technical and functional aspects of products and processes. You can apply for a patent if your product is new and inventive. Look for other similar ideas through the free online search of registered patents at *http://gb.espacenet.com* before you apply. The process can take a number of years and involves various payments at the different stages. Prepare a description of your product, drawings, claims for what it does, and a technical summary before you fill in the initial application forms on the UKIPO site. You may then be asked to improve the product information and send in prototypes, all of which can add to your costs.

Whichever you opt for remember that patents and registered designs only apply to a single country and you may need to go through the process internationally too.

Once you have a clear idea in your head about your product, it is time to try it out on other people. Get people to sign a non-disclosure agreement as you don't want word to get out before you are ready to launch. Then work out the best way to find the views of potential customers on your products and prices. Choose from:

- One to one interviews – face to face or over the phone.
- Focus groups – ideally six to eight people in a room.
- Surveys – use a printed or online survey to reach large numbers of people.

When you have a solid base of research feed this into the start of a plan for your business. It will all help when you start to work out pricing, promote to the media, contact retailers or market to customers.

Next, you will need to look for manufacturers. This can be a long process and may involve some trial and error until you find a company with the correct equipment in a good location who can provide the right sort of quality at a suitable price.

At the same time you will need to start looking for potential retailers in order to make sure you can sell your product as soon as it is available. Back this up with marketing, advertising and PR. You'll see that there is a lot to think about if you want to invent your own product.

If you're serious about getting your idea to market, Cally Robson advises, "The fail rate is high. It's estimated that only 2% of concepts actually make it to the market. But for those that do, if they hit the right spot, such as Lisa Irlam's Pool-mate lap counter for swimmers, annual profits can be in the millions.

"There are many pitfalls and traps for newbie product entrepreneurs along the way, and not just known scams from invention marketing companies that take your money and do little in return. Unfortunately the nature of the industry lends itself to designing and protecting products and inventions with little regard to whether it will be commercially viable. For that reason, it's best to hook up with a network of people who've done it already and can steer you around the pitfalls and put you in touch with trusted professionals."

Further information

- She's Ingenious! - *www.shesingenious.org* - the only website packed with information and support for women developing and marketing new products and inventions BY women who've done it themselves.

- The British Library Business & IP Centre in London - *www.bl.uk/bipc* - or your nearest Patent & Business library – see listing at *www.epo.org/patents/ patent-information/patlib/directory/unitedkingdom.html*

- Your local Business Link – Their specialist innovation centre or services - *http://online.businesslink.gov.uk*

- The Chartered Institute of Patent Attorneys - *www.cipa.org.uk*

- GWIIN - The Global Women Innovators and Inventors Network - *www.gwiin.com*

- The Intellectual Property Office (IPO) - *www.ipo.gov.uk*

- Lawyers4Mumpreneurs – for legal advice including non disclosure agreements - *www.lawyers4mumpreneurs.com*

- A local inventor's group (but beware, they are traditionally very male) – Wessex Round Table of Inventors have the most complete listing I've come across at *www.wrti.org.uk/clubs*

- Sorcit – for professional help with product development *www.sorcitproducts.com*

- For more excellent advice about protecting your business ideas, check out *The Bright Ideas Handbook* by Michael Gardner (Which? Books)

You might also like
- ❑ Online shop

Other Business Ideas Beginning with 'I'
- ❑ Interior Designer
- ❑ Iridology
- ❑ Ironing
- ❑ Image consultant

JOURNALIST

What is it?

A journalist writes for newspapers, magazines and websites. In this article we focus on freelance journalism: employed work as a journalist is usually NOT family friendly.

Tell me more...

Many people dream of writing for a living, and while an employed job in journalism often comes with unrealistically long hours for many mums, freelance work can allow you to do something you love and be around for the family.

What are the benefits?

You get to research interesting ideas, write them up and see them published. You can do this at any time of the day (or night). Writing for a living is never an easy option, and is often poorly paid, but if you enjoy writing it can be incredibly rewarding.

Things to consider...

If you want to write for a living, it can help if you have specialist expertise as it can be highly competitive. If you were an accountant, think about writing on financial matters, for example. Developing a niche can give editors a compelling reason to use you.

You will need to research the publications you want to write for to see they sort of articles they use, then come up with a pitch – a couple of hundred words outlining your idea, why the publication's readers will be interested, and why you are well placed to write it. You will now need to find the right person to send your pitch to on each publication. Send it in, then follow up with a phone call. Don't be deterred if your first ideas don't get accepted: you need to persist in order to build relationships with editors and get regular work.

Rates of pay vary and even the biggest publications are struggling with budgets. It is a competitive area to get into which also drives down pay.

Be open-minded about the sort of writing you want to do. There are thousands of small businesses in need of help with copywriting and this sort of work can be easier to fit round the family than dealing with stressed and demanding editors on tight deadlines.

There are also hundreds of internet publications looking for content. This can be a good way to get started but many pay low rates and beware of those that don't pay at all!

Further information
- Check out the NUJ Rate for the Job site at *http://media.gn.apc.org/rates* which gives you a good idea of how much to ask for at a wide range of publications.

Books:
- *Commercial writing: How to earn a living as a business writer* by Antonia Chitty (Hale Books) - This book explains all about the business of writing and gives you lots of ideas to build your business on, whether you want to write for magazines, do online copywriting, or write for marketing materials.

Websites:
- *www.journobiz.com*
- *www.journalism.co.uk*
- *www.freelancewritingtips.com* - no longer updated but still full of good advice

You might also like
- ❑ Copywriting
- ❑ Public Relations
- ❑ Marketing
- ❑ Editor and proofreader

Other Business Ideas Beginning with 'J'
- ❑ Jewellery maker

KITCHEN CLEANER
(AND HELP WITH OTHER HOUSEHOLD TASKS)

What is it?

Helping clients to take care of their homes, gardens and pets.

Tell me more...

People often want help with these tasks around their homes:

- Cleaning
- Oven valeting
- Gardening
- Ironing
- Pet sitting
- Dog walking
- Window cleaning

Your clients could be busy working people, over stretched mums and, as older people now want to stay in their own homes for as long as they can, demand for this type of service could well be on the increase.

What are the benefits?

- This type of business is usually simple, cheap and quick to get started (although getting a steady stream of clients will usually take some time, planning and effort).

- You can work as many hours work as you want.

- You can choose to offer as many of the different services (listed above) as you want.

- If you get too much work for you alone, you could employ other people.

Things to consider...

Word-of-mouth is a very effective way of finding clients for this type of business. Make sure your friends, family and neighbours all know about your service so they can refer people to you. Even better, get some business cards printed and leave a few with all your family and friends so they can pass them on.

Agree with your clients exactly what you are going to do and when. Will you be using your own materials and tools (e.g. cleaning products, lawn mower) or theirs? Which cleaning tasks will you do in the time you are working for your client? This helps you avoid disagreements later on.

You could try to think of a way to stand out from other businesses in your area. How about using only eco-friendly products?

Because these types of business are quick to set up, it could be easy to overlook the basics of starting a business. For example, make sure you get adequate insurance as you could accidentally break a client's window, stain her carpet or burn an item of clothing with an iron. If you're offering an ironing service, will you need a heavy-duty iron and ironing board to avoid replacing your ordinary one frequently? Also, don't forget you will need to register as self employed with HMRC and, if your earnings are above a certain level, pay tax and national insurance.

Further information

- *www.startagardeningbusiness.co.uk* - a website on starting a gardening business
- *www.windowcleaningcoach.com* - a down-to-earth guide to starting a window cleaning business from Dave the window cleaning coach
- There are several franchises available for cleaning companies. You can check them out at sites like *www.franchisedirect.co*.uk and *www.whichfranchise.com*
- Register as self employed at *www.hmrc.co.uk*

You might also like
❑ Painting and Decorating

Other Business Ideas Beginning with 'K'
❑ Knitting
❑ Kinesiologist
❑ Kennel Owner

LIFE COACH

What is it?
Helping clients to obtain what they want in their lives.

Tell me more...
A coach listens intently to understand what is important to her client and what may be holding her back. The coach helps the client to define her goals then works with the client to make sure she takes the steps to achieve those goals.

What are the benefits?
- You can choose how many hours you work
- You can work from home by phone
- You can branch out into other areas such as writing and running workshops

Things to consider...
Coaching is a difficult service to sell, especially if you have no experience in marketing. It's not easy to describe what the client will get or what the end result will be. If you decide to begin a coaching business, allow for a lot (often more than 50%) of your time to be spent on marketing in the first few years.

The good news is that you can work over the phone from anywhere. The bad news is that you're competing with every other coach in the world who can do the same! It's highly unlikely that you'll be able to build a business as a general coach – you will need to specialise. When choosing your specialism, make sure you pick one with clients that can afford to pay for your services. For example, people who have just lost their jobs may need your services, but they probably won't have the money to pay for you.

Could you build a coaching business on the skills and experience you already have? If you have a marketing background you could coach business owners on marketing, for example. Other options might be becoming a writing, PR or weight-loss coach.

Before paying for a coach training course, investigate the training provider and course thoroughly. While many are reputable, there is nothing to stop anyone starting a coach training company, so it pays to do your homework. Courses come in a variety of lengths and prices, so weigh up exactly what you want from a course and if you're getting value for money. Ask to speak to recent students who have successful coaching businesses.

Further information

Examples of coaches who have specialisms:
- *www.thedivorcedoctor.co.uk* - relationship coaching
- *www.candocanbe.com* - marketing coaching for small business owners

Some coach training organisations (there are others):
- *www.noble-manhattan.com*
- *www.the-coaching-academy.com*
- *www.thecoaches.com*
- *www.coachinc.com*

Coaching information and resources:
- *www.coachville.com* - resources for coaches, some free
- *www.lifecoach-directory.org.uk* – aimed at people looking for a life coach, but check out the FAQ page for helpful description of what coaches do, plus the experience and qualifications they need.
- *www.newcoachconnection.com* – a Yahoo group supporting new coaches

You might also like

- ❏ Teacher
- ❏ Trainer
- ❏ Teaching Assistant
- ❏ Business Coach

Other Business Ideas Beginning with 'L'

- ❏ Leatherwork

MAGAZINE OWNER

What is it?

Editing, publishing and distributing a local magazine.

Tell me more...

You can start a business that produces a magazine for your town or local area. You would earn money by selling advertising space in the magazine.

- You can either buy a franchise or start your own magazine from scratch

- Your magazine could be aimed at anyone in the local area or could be for a specific group of people like parents or business people

What are the benefits?

- You can choose your working hours to fit around your family

- The satisfaction of producing your own magazine

- The potential to earn a decent income from a part-time business, although it will probably take several years of hard work to get there

Things to consider...

You will probably have a heavy workload on the run up to the publication deadline. How will this fit with your family commitments? Can someone else handle the childcare if you need them to?

You'll have to chase some advertisers for payment. You'll need to be persistent and not afraid of phoning people and asking for the money you are owed. It may take a while to get payment, so you'll need to make sure you can survive if several advertisers don't pay up for a few months.

You will need computer skills to put together the magazine, plus specialist software and a computer that is up to the job.

When researching franchises, check if training and software is included.

If you're not going down the franchise route and are starting your own magazine, advertisers may be reluctant to part with their money as you won't have a track record. Before you approach advertisers, think about how you can convince them that their advert will reach their potential customers. You could put together a prototype showing how the magazine will look, for example. Explain how you will make sure that your magazines are distributed properly. E.g. by phoning a sample of recipients to make sure their magazine arrived.

If you're considering buying a franchise, check out this book's section on franchising. Some magazine franchises claim that you can earn a good living from just a few hours work each month. Don't take the franchiser's word for this - talk to someone who is already running a community magazine.

Franchisers will often give you exclusive rights to an area, but this doesn't stop someone starting a rival magazine from another franchise or an independent magazine in your area. When doing your research, check out your competition, there may already be several magazines in your area.

Further information

Some franchises that you can buy are:

- *www.getraring2go.co.uk*
- *www.mycommunitytimes.co.uk*
- *www.thefamilygrapevine.co.uk*

Reading:

- *www.ousevalleyliving.com* is an independent (i.e. not a franchise) community magazine - check out their website for inspiration.

You might also like
❑   Online store
❑   Website Owner (information)

Other Business Ideas Beginning with 'M'
❑   Manufacturer
❑   Making soap and other bath products
❑   Marketer
❑   Massage Therapy & Bodywork
❑   Meditation
❑   Model making
❑   Music Class leader
❑   Mystery Shopper

NAIL TECHNICIAN
(AND OTHER BEAUTY THERAPIES)

What is it?

Helping clients to look and feel great.

Tell me more...

Do you enjoy working with people and have an interest in beauty? Then you might like...

- Beauty therapy
- Spray tanning
- Manicure and pedicure
- Facials
- Massage

What are the benefits?

You can work as many hours as you want. Some clients may actually prefer you to work in the evenings and at weekends, which can fit well around a family.

If you've always had a passion for beauty, this could be your chance to turn it into a career.

Things to consider...

You can work from home, visit your clients in their homes or hire a room in a hairdressing or beauty salon. You could combine working in different venues to reach a range of clients and see which is most successful for you. If you rent a room, you will still need to market your services. The centre or salon owner may help you to do this, but on its own this will not be enough to bring you a steady stream of clients.

Marketing methods that work well for this type of business are either word-of-mouth or 'taster' sessions. There's nothing like a referral from a happy customer or a chance to demonstrate how good you are.

It's a good idea to have a website listing your services, but this needn't cost as much as you think. Health Hosts (*www.healthhosts.com*) have website packages for therapists that start at £4.95 per month.

You might like to consider packaging your services. For example, devise a bridal package that gives the bride-to-be all the treatments she needs to look fabulous on her big day. Perhaps you could offer a mum-to-be package for pregnant clients or even a 'fabulous over 50' package. Other possibilities are offering pampering parties or hen nights.

Link up with beauty or hairdressing colleagues to create inclusive packages and pass on referrals.

If you're working from home, check with your local authority's environmental health department as they may need to inspect your working area. Don't forget to inform your home insurance company that you're running a business from home. You'll also need to consider the implications of bringing clients to your home. Do clients need to walk through your home to reach your treatment room? If so, will you be able to maintain a professional image with children around? Even if you work evenings when they are in bed, you may still have to deal with the mess they leave behind!

Make sure you have adequate insurance for the services you're providing.

Further information
- ITEC - *www.itecworld.co.uk* - offers a range of beauty therapy qualifications plus a new business qualification
- *www.healthypages.co.uk* - has a list of courses and a forum covering a wide range of therapies
- Or check out your local college

You might also like
- ❏ Hairdresser
- ❏ Complementary therapist
- ❏ Make Up artist

Other Business Ideas Beginning with 'N'
- ❏ Naturopath
- ❏ Nutritionist

ONLINE STORE

What is it?
Selling goods, or sometimes services, over the internet.

Tell me more...
Running an online store allows you to sell goods over the internet.

What are the benefits?
- This is a great flexible job as you can work at the times that suit you

- The internet allows you to develop a niche business and reach potential customers regardless of their location

Things to consider...
Nikki Backshall is an Ecommerce expert. She runs Webmums which offers online training at *www.webmums.com*. Nikki explains, "The term Ecommerce refers to the sale of any product online – from digital media to physical goods. Online buying is a multi-billion dollar industry with ripe pickings for Mumpreneurs with a bit of savvy. As technology improves and the Internet becomes more widely used, it's a tangible business model for anyone wanting to work from home."

There are many things to consider if you are going into Ecommerce. Nikki advises, "It is a learning process that needs to be continued. If you put up an online shop and expect it just to 'sell' something you'll be disappointed: it isn't that straight-forward. There are some basics that you will need to get started. To really pack a punch I'd urge you to learn about SEO (Search Engine Optimisation) and also how social media can have a huge impact on the success of your online store."

To get you started, Nikki suggests, "Always begin with market research. There is little point selling something that nobody wants even if *you* think it will sell. Use free tools like

Google's keyword tool to find out exactly what people are searching for. Speak to and survey real people and ask them if they think your product is viable. Family and friends will tell you what you want to hear so make sure that you speak to people who will give you genuine feedback. Don't be put off by competition: if there is competition then it's a thriving market – you just need to rise above the noise and become the market leader."

Once you have established a viable market for your products you'll need to have your shop built. Nikki explains, "There are many ecommerce platforms that you can use. Some are free (known as open source). This is good in theory but it does take some technical know-how to install, build and maintain your own online store. You can hire someone to do this for you depending on your budget. I'd personally recommend a hosted shopping cart with an easy build interface. EKM Power shop is a good example of this although there are many others. Don't skimp on your research at this stage this as changing e-commerce platforms is a real headache so it's best to get it right first."

Once your shop is up and running there are some simple things you can do to increase your success. It will be a gradual process to work out how to drive sufficient visitors to your site and to learn how to convert browsers to buyers. Follow the points below from Nikki for a great start:

- Make use of great images on your home page and product pages. Images sell better than words and if they look blurry or unprofessional then it will be incredibly detrimental. Equally, professional pictures will increase your conversion rate substantially.
- Keep it simple! Everything needs to be user friendly, including the shopping cart. Don't ask your customer for a ton of details and to fill out endless forms. Most won't! Take the details you need to fulfil their order and nothing more.

- If you are selling the same item in different sizes then you don't need individual pages for each size. Give your customer the opportunity to choose the size and the colour from the page they are on. This is easier for your customer, and protects you against the risk that they assume you don't have the item in other colours or sizes and go elsewhere. Make sure you choose a shopping cart that has this facility available.

- Make use of the opportunity to cross sell: check that cross selling, upselling and back end offers are available options when you choose your cart. You can make a huge addition to your bottom line with these techniques (depending on the market that you are in).

- Make sure that you have an opt-in box for customers to subscribe to your newsletter and make customers aware of your newsletter at every opportunity. It's far easier to sell to an existing customer than it is to generate new ones. Sign up to a reputable email client and get that opt-in box on your storefront in anticipation of sending out a newsletter each month.

- Accept vouchers in-store. You can use a voucher system to encourage people to sign up to your newsletter – say 10% discount on their first purchase. You can also use them for promotions, lead generations and competitions. Again, check that this is something that your cart provider includes within their features.

- Make sure that you accept more than one payment type, with PayPal and Google checkout being amongst them. The more options that you give, the more sales you will make.

- Make use of the payment thank you page! One of the biggest oversights in ecommerce is the complete waste of the 'thank you' page. If someone has just bought from you then they are in 'buying mode' and it is at this point when they are most likely to buy from you again. Use this page to showcase other products and have a sign up box for your newsletter or a special offer for new customers. The possibilities are endless here – so again, check to see if there is something within the software of your cart that will allow you to add something to your 'thank you' page after your customer has purchased from you.

- Make sure your cart / store platform allows customer reviews. It's been proven time and time again that reviews sell. I'm sure you've seen the success proven on major shopping sites like Amazon and it's also good feedback for you too. If you have a product that is getting continuous bad feedback then you know to drop this from your inventory. On the flip side, products receiving rave reviews can be featured for extra sales. In addition, it also adds fresh content to your site and Google loves fresh content.

- Familiarize yourself with search engine optimisation – that's using key words and phrases to draw people in to your site from search engines. It's an art and the more you learn the better you'll get. You might be interested to know that almost 15% of online searches in Google are retail related, so it's imperative that you know how to get your store indexed and ranking highly. Learning about keyword research will help you to find out what people are searching for and how you can get your biz in front of their eyeballs.

- Regularly review and tweak you main sales copy. It's good to keep things fresh for the search engines – and it's good for you to test what is working and what isn't. Plus you should be adapting to seasonal promotions and keeping things new and fresh for your returning customers (you know, the ones that receive your newsletter and come back when you email them to tell them what's new in store!).

- Give GREAT customer service – this one thing alone will stand you head and shoulders above most of your competition. In a world where great customer service is so easily over-looked, it makes it a no-brainer to make this a top priority for you. Besides, if you can't give the kind of service that you would personally like to receive yourself, then an ecommerce biz isn't right for you. Make sure that you don't just meet your customers' needs, you need to make them sit up and say 'wow'.

- Get yourself a blog! This is a must for online businesses nowadays and a great way to promote your business. You can even build your estore on a WordPress.org blog if you have the know-how and that can be a great money saver. This is especially good for hobby and craft sites or businesses that are only selling a few products. If you are selling a huge variety of products – I'd recommend a shopping cart with a blog on the side.

- Learn about social media and how you can use it to influence the success of your business. Powerful sites like Twitter can make a huge difference and the Internet is becoming more and more 'social based' as we move into the Web 2.0 world of business to customer interaction. There are right ways and very wrong ways to use these sites so make sure you've done your homework before venturing into them.

An ecommerce business can be a great business for a mum but it is time consuming. A site can be built on a fairly low budget, but it can't be built for free. It takes time, commitment and some financial investment to get your online business up and running properly, so make sure that you have properly researched your market and the best shopping cart before going ahead.

Join some communities where you can network with some other Mumpreneurs as there are always opportunities for joint ventures and cross promotion of businesses, plus there is a wealth of information from these women who are always more than happy to share their own knowledge and experiences of working online.

Further information

- *www.webmums.com* – courses to help you get to grips with the internet

There are innumerable sites that make it simple for you to create your own store, or you can get a designer to create one for you:

- Actinic - *www.actinic.co.uk*
- EKMPowerShop - *www.ekmpowershop.com*
- Moonfruit - *www.moonfruit.co.uk*
- Mr Site - *www.mrsite.co.uk*
- Oscommerce - *www.oscommerce.com*
- Romancart - *www.romancart.com*
- Store2go - *www.store2go.net*
- Zencart - *www.zencart.co.uk*

Newsletter providers:

- Constant Contact - *www.constantcontact.com*
- Just Add Content - *www.justaddcontent.co.uk*
- AWeber - *www.aweber.com*
- Vertical Response - *www.verticalresponse.com*

You might also like

❑ Website owner

Other Business Ideas Beginning with 'O'

❑ Osteopath
❑ Optician or optometrist

PARTY PLANNER

What is it?

Direct selling is selling a product for commission on a self-employed basis. Parties are just one way of direct selling.

What is it?

Direct selling can be done by holding a party, distributing catalogues door-to-door, selling direct to friends and family or holding a stall at a fete or craft fair. Products include toiletries, cosmetics, kitchen/cooking equipment, children's toys, clothes and books, cleaning products and even utilities. Well known names include Avon, Kleeneze, Usborne Books, Body Shop at Home and many more.

Some companies encourage reps to build their own teams and you may already have been approached by someone hoping to recruit you onto their team. The team leaders are sometimes known as 'uplines'. There's a financial incentive to recruit reps, perhaps a higher rate of commission or a payment each time a team member places an order.

What are the benefits?

- It's usually cheap and easy to get started compared to starting your own business from scratch.

- Catalogues, leaflets and other marketing materials are produced by the company, so you don't have to do this yourself.

- Often companies don't give you any targets or pressure to sell. But check this to be sure.

- You don't need any business experience.

- It can fit in around caring for children. You might host parties during the day or push a buggy around the neighbourhood distributing catalogues. Or you could host parties in the evening when the children are in bed.

Things to consider...

Money

How much money will you actually make? If you ask this question of your recruiter they will probably, quite rightly, tell you that it depends on how hard you work - although any previous experience of selling, your personality, your feelings about the product and the geographical area you work in will be factors too. So you'll need to do a few simple calculations yourself.

Let's say that you host a party and your takings are £200. You get 25% commission, so you think you have made £50. But you may then have to pay for catalogues, order forms, postage to have the products sent to you, petrol to deliver the goods to your customers, tax and national insurance plus nibbles and drinks for the party. (You might not have to pay for all of this as different companies work in different ways.)

So let's say you actually earn £35 for the party - how many parties will you need to host to make the income you need (e.g. per week or month)? How many hours work will it take you to host the parties, get party bookings, place orders then sort and distribute the goods when they arrive?

If you're distributing catalogues door-to-door, how many people will need to place an order and how much will the average order amount need to be for you to earn the income you want? How much time will it take you to cover this area?

Having done the maths, will you be able to make the income you need from selling the product alone? Or will you need to recruit a team of your own? Recruiting a team is a different prospect from selling the product - do you have skills? If not, could you learn them? Do you want to have your own team?

Find out if there are any sales targets. Some people are motivated by targets, others loathe them. Which one are you? Does the company match you, your family commitments and the way you want to run this business?

Your team leader

How experienced is your prospective team leader? And what level of support will they give you? Once you have signed up with a team leader you may not be allowed to change to another, so it pays to ask what level of support you can expect beforehand. Many companies encourage new reps to get recruiting straight away, so you may find yourself with a team leader with only one week more experience than you! If you're a complete beginner at selling and party plans, it could be really helpful to pick someone with lots of experience who is able and willing to share that experience with you.

You could even ask the team leader how much money they make a month. This will give you an idea of the potential of the business and the success of your team leader. If they give you a figure, make sure you know exactly what this is - is it the takings from their parties, their commission and if they've subtracted their expenses and tax/national insurance or not?

The product

Make sure you love the product. It's an uphill struggle convincing people to buy something when you don't one hundred percent believe in it.

Is the product a) good quality and b) favourably priced compared to similar (or the same) products in the shops or online? It is tough trying to sell a product that people can buy in the supermarket next time they do the weekly shop. Especially if it's cheaper in the supermarket! The products sold by party plan are usually very good quality, but that often makes them more expensive – will your customers be prepared to pay extra for this quality?

Competitors

Find out how many other reps for this company are there in your area. You'll stand a better chance of party bookings if people haven't already been approached by three reps from the same company as you. But it can be tough to find out how many reps there are in your area, because it's often a free-for-all. Some reps will be signed up with the company but might not be active, so even the company itself may not be able to give you very useful information. Instead, you could try looking in the places reps might be (e.g. school fairs), checking local websites or asking around your friends to see if they have been asked to host a party or have had catalogues through their doors.

Paying tax and national insurance

You will be self-employed so responsible for paying your own tax and national insurance. You will also need to keep records as evidence of what you have earned and your business expenses.

If you're not making much money then you may not reach the threshold for paying income tax and national insurance, but you will still need to inform HRMC that you are self employed within 3 months of starting work to avoid paying a fine.

For more information

- Direct Selling Association - *www.dsa.org.uk*

- The Direct Selling and Party Plan Directory at *www.familyfriendlyworking.co.uk* has a list of party plan companies

- The 'working for yourself and self employed chat club' at the *www.netmums.com* Coffee House has a thread for many direct selling schemes and party plans

- *www.businessopportunitywatch.com* reviews home-based business opportunities

- Go to *www.hmrc.gov.uk* to register as self employed.

You might also like

❑ Online Store Owner
❑ Drop Shipper

Other Business Ideas Beginning with 'P'

❑ Painting
❑ Personal trainer
❑ Pets and animal care
❑ Photographer
❑ Potter
❑ Project manager
❑ Psychotherapy
❑ Public Relations
❑ Proof reader

RUNNING A BUSINESS

What is it?

If you're reading this book you're one of the many mums thinking about running a business. Whatever your background, it is possible to learn to run a business but there are some key areas to think about first. The elements that make a successful business apply whatever sort of business you plan.

Tell me more...

To create a successful business you need more than just a good idea. Have you thought about your skills in business planning, finance, marketing, PR, advertising and sales? You'll need to have a plan for how you can carry out all these functions ... and probably answer the phone and make the tea too.

What are the benefits?

Running a business gives you ultimate control over how and when you work. You can decide to have a small business that brings in pocket money, one that allows you to pay for family holidays and extras, or a business that is the main source of income for your family. Be clear about your business goals and you can develop your plans accordingly.

If you become a business owner, though, you will find that you need to learn a range of new skills. Be clear about where your strengths lie and where you might need further training or to get help in.

Things to consider...

Planning

Have you thought about a plan for your business? Creating a business plan is essential if you want to borrow money to start the business, and even if you are financing it yourself you will find that planning pays dividends. Think of your business plan like a map. Create a vision for where you would like your business to be in five years time. Your plan should show you the steps you need to take to reach your destination. If you are unsure about business planning your local enterprise agency is likely to offer training to help you get started, and we have created a guide to help you start thinking about your plans at the back of the book.

Practicalities

Work out how you will run your business on a day-to-day basis. Ask yourself questions like:

- Where will I work?
- How will I get stock manufactured?
- How will I store my stock?
- Where will I pick and pack?
- Can I do all the post office runs, do I need help or should I look into couriers?
- Will I work by myself, outsource some work to freelancers or take on staff?

These and many more questions will depend on your exact business and situation, so start putting down your answers in a notebook or in a plan online.

Finance

What are your finance skills like? Running a business requires a willingness to get to grips with the figures ... otherwise your business can turn into an expensive hobby. Look at every cost you incur in getting the business started. Estimate the ongoing costs such as utilities, ink and paper, rent, business rates and utilities if you have premises, a website, PR, marketing and advertising too. All these need to be factored into the final cost of your product. Calculate an hourly rate to pay yourself: you may not be able to pay yourself much when you start but if you don't factor this in you can end up working for nothing. Again, go to the back of the book to find a handy guide to help you start thinking about your business finances, and find more help in *The Mumpreneur Guide's Start Your Own Business* Book by Antonia Chitty.

INSURANCE

Insurance is vital for any business, but what sort of insurance will you need? Think about whether you need to cover your equipment, stock, people visiting your premises, the public using your products or people attending your events.

- Public liability insurance is necessary if clients come to your premises. This covers legal fees, costs and expenses and damages if someone is injured while in your office.

- Employers' insurance: employer's liability compulsory insurance to meet the costs of compensation and legal fees for employees who are injured or made ill at work through the fault of the employer. You do not need this insurance if you are the only employee of a company, or if you are a self employed sole trader.

- Buildings insurance

- Equipment insurance: if you use equipment solely for business use you may need business insurance cover. Check with your own insurance provider. A business property policy can offer insurance for your equipment, fixtures and fittings, plus cover for leased equipment and client's property.

- Professional indemnity insurance: this policy protects you if you have made mistakes or have been negligent in some of the services you provide to clients. It will cover you for legal costs and compensation. You need to arrange cover before you start work, and need to ensure that your cover is continuous, so you have cover for when the problem occurred, and when the client actually makes the claim, which may be years down the line.

Online Business

Few businesses can manage without a website, and many mum-owned businesses are only practical because of how the internet can put you in touch with niche audiences and allow you to take orders and handle enquiries while looking after the family. So, develop a plan for how your business will grow online. Think about whether you can create a simple site to start the business off, or whether you need a web developer to help you. Start looking into *www.twitter.com* and *www.facebook.com* as ways of developing a following. If you offer business-to-business products or services look at *www.linkedin.com* or *www.ecademy.com*. And make sure your site has an integrated blog as this can help you add fresh content on a regular basis and appear more highly in search engine results.

Promotion

Have you thought about how you will market your product or service? Create a marketing plan, and think about public relations, advertising, and sales campaigns too. Be clear about your potential customers for a start. Write down as much about them as you can: their age, gender, where they shop, how they earn money, how they communicate, what they read or watch. This will make it easier to understand how to reach them. Look at your budget for promoting your business and plan how you might spend it over the year. In your first year of business you may make some mistakes, but that's inevitable. Just note down what promotion you do, how much it costs and how much time it takes and track where your customers come from. That way you'll be able to work out what works well for your business. Keep a list of new promotion ideas, things that you see other businesses doing perhaps, and add them into your plan too. If you're short on ideas there are some free downloads at *www.prbasics.co.uk* or buy Antonia Chitty's Guide to *Promoting Your Business* which is designed for business owners on a budget.

Further information

Books designed for mums starting a business:

- *Family Friendly Working* by Antonia Chitty
- *Kitchen Table Tycoon* by Anita Naik
- *Make It Your Business* by Lucy Martin & Bella Mehta
- *Millionaire Mumpreneur* by Mel McGee
- *Mum Ultrapreneur* by Susan Odev & Mark Weeks
- *Supermummy* - Mel McGee
- *The Mumpreneur Guide* by Antonia Chitty

Business and Enterprise Organisations:

- Business Link, England - *www.businesslink.gov.uk* - 0845 6009006
- Business Support, Wales - *www.business-support-wales.gov.uk* - 03000 6 03000
- Venture Wales - *www.venturewales.com* - 0845 0453150
- Welsh Assembly Government - *http://new.wales.gov.uk/topics/businessandeconomy*
- Highlands and Islands Enterprise, Scotland - *www.hie.co.uk* - 01463 234171
- Business Gateway, Scotland - *www.bgateway.com*
- Scottish Enterprise - *www.scottish-enterprise.com* - 0845 6078787 (Scotland) 0141 228 2000 (UK)
- Scottish Development International - *www.scotent.co.uk* - 0141 228 2828
- Invest Northern Ireland - *www.investni.com* - 028 9023 9090

General business websites:

- www.aardvarkbusiness.net
- www.enterprisenation.com
- www.smallbusinesssuccess.biz

- www.startupdonut.co.uk
- www.startups.co.uk
- www.ukbusinessforums.co.uk

Women's business websites:

- www.auroravoice.com
- www.everywoman.co.uk/networking
- www.giantpotential.ning.com
- www.motheratwork.co.uk
- www.womenatwork.co.uk

Other Business Ideas Beginning with 'R'

❑ Reiki master
❑ Recruitment
❑ Reflexologist
❑ Researcher
❑ Running a cafe

SELLING...

What is it?

Selling is something that every mum who wants to own a business of any sort has to embrace. You may have the best business idea on the world, but you will still need to sell it to people. And selling is essential whether you offer products or services.

Tell me more...

Many mums are passionate about their businesses but feel shy when it comes to selling. The sooner you embrace your inner sales woman the sooner your business will turn a profit.

What are the benefits?

If you believe that what you are offering has value for your customers, this should help you develop the confidence to sell it to them. Work out what is unique and special about your product and service, and practise telling this to potential customers. Don't just tell them about the 'features' of what you offer, but tell them about the benefits and how you can help them solve a problem, get results or change their lives.

Things to consider...

Laura Rigney of *www.pitcherhouse.co.uk* has 11 years experience in sales, covering telesales, field sales and marketing sales. She helps businesses improve their sales techniques and has the following advice for mums who feel their sales skills need a boost:

Ask Questions. If you ask the right questions you can tailor your product to any company. You need your prospect to be able to see the benefits of them stocking your product or using your service. This is the best time to use your USP. Example:

Seller: What kind of customers are you looking to attract?

Buyer: We mainly target families with young children.

Seller: Excellent! Our brochure is distributed through various soft play areas, local/national maternity units and toddler groups. So you can see that we are hitting your target market on your behalf, can't you?

Buyer: Yes.

Once you have given the buyer the answer they want to hear, affirm it. Make sure they agree with what you've said. This is key to success!

Laura continues, "Don't try to sell via email. An MD or a marketing director will open an email, realise that it is a sales pitch and delete, simple as that. The most effective forms of sales are telesales or field sales. This allows you to build a relationship with your prospect which is vital! People want to buy from people, not emails. An additional benefit is that this allows you to gauge whether there is any genuine interest in your product."

If you are unsure what to say when making a sales call, write yourself a script. This can help you remember some of the key benefits you need to highlight and as you warm up you will find yourself more able to improvise, with the security of having some guidance on the page in front of you should you need. When creating your script or making a call, Laura advises, "Be direct. When trying to sell something, be straight to the point. People get numerous calls every day of the week trying to convince them to buy something. The more you skirt around the edges trying to avoid asking the important questions, the more uninterested they become. This doesn't mean introducing yourself and then asking for money. Simply explain who you are, what you are selling and why it would be beneficial to your prospect. Once they see the benefit to them they have no reason to say no."

If you're terrified of telephoning, you're not alone. Lots of mums start businesses based largely on email communications and with small children this is sometimes the only practical way to do it. However, if you have a fear of the telephone, recognise that this could hold your business back and work out what you could do to overcome your fears. Look at the benefits of making calls, and find an incentive that will motivate you to make a single business call. Then, build up gradually.

If you have a product and want to make contact with potential retailers, make sure you speak to the right person. Laura suggests, "The single most important thing to remember when trying to establish contact with a company is to speak to the correct person. This needs to be the MAN – the person with:

- Money
- Authority
- Need

Your contact must have complete control of the organisations purse strings, the authority to sign off payments and the need to buy from you. You could do the world's best pitch to a buying or marketing assistant and have them totally convinced that they need to buy from you. However, when they go and relay this information to the MAN they WILL miss out vital details that you would always include. This means that the person with the buying power never gets your full pitch and will never truly understand your product." She adds, "The majority of the time, the person that you need to speak to will be the first person to arrive and the last person to leave their business. Use this knowledge wisely. Instead of calling them at 10am when they are likely to be in a meeting / on a conference call etc, call them between 8am - 9am or 5pm - 6pm. If you are lucky enough to get them on the phone, they will have more time to focus on you and the reason for your call rather than hurrying you off the line."

Further information

- *www.salesandmarketingforums.co.uk*
- *www.getclientsnow.com*

You might also like

❑ PR
❑ Marketing

Other Business Ideas Beginning with 'S'

❑ Seamstress – clothes, nappies, baby carriers
❑ Selling collectibles
❑ Selling craft supplies
❑ Selling food
❑ Selling handmade crafts and art
❑ Shamanisim
❑ Shiatsu
❑ Shop owner
❑ Soft toy maker
❑ Spray Tanner
❑ Stallholder

TUTOR

What is it?
If you enjoy working with children, you could tutor them outside school hours in subjects such as maths and English.

Tell me more...
- You can either work for an agency, find your own clients or both.

- You can work in your own home or in your clients' homes, although it's usually more cost effective to work from your own home as it saves travelling time and expenses.

- You can work with individuals or small groups, primary school children or secondary.

What are the benefits?
- You can choose how many hours you work

- You can work weekends and evenings

- It's very satisfying work if you enjoy teaching but find the thought of being a classroom teacher too bureaucratic or stressful.

- If you have the right qualifications, you could combine tutoring with related work such as exam invigilation, online tutoring or marking exams.

Things to consider...
Make sure you really enjoy working with children!

Teaching methods will almost certainly have changed since you were at school. Unless you've been a teacher very recently, you'll need to learn how your subject is taught in schools now if you're going to avoid confusing your clients. You may find it easier to work with children who attend the same school because you'll have only one syllabus to work with.

Remember to allow at least half an hour's preparation for each hour of tutoring.

Although there's no legal requirement, parents will usually want you to be CRB (Criminal Records Bureau) checked. You can't apply for a CRB check as an individual or self employed person, so you'll need to get this through an organisation. You could do this by signing up with a tutoring agency, although they may make you pay for this. Or you could do some voluntary work, such as running an after-school club at a local school. This would also give you useful experience and may help you make some contacts.

If you're signing up with an agency, look for one that advertises regularly in the area where you want to work. You can advertise in your local paper, by putting up a card in local shop windows, on free websites such as *www.gumtree.com*. You can also send your details to local schools - if parents ask for teachers for extra tuition, they may pass on your details. Once you get started, you should be able to get work by word-of-mouth referrals, so make sure you have some business cards printed that clients can hand out to friends.

Be clear about your expectations when you sign up a new client - how much notice do you need for cancellation? What happens if the child doesn't do their homework? What materials do you provide? What happens if you or the child is late for a session?

You don't necessarily need a teaching qualification, although this is a big advantage. The need for a teaching qualification will often depend on supply and demand in your area. E.g. if there aren't enough qualified maths teachers to go around then you may be able to find maths tutoring work without a teaching qualification

There isn't a steady stream of work throughout the year - work increases on the run up to exams and decreases over the summer holidays.

Further information

Agencies and other websites where you can find work:

- *www.aplustutors.co.uk*
- *www.personal-tutors.co.uk*
- *www.firstclasslearning.co.uk*
- *www.thetutorpages.com*
- *www.beanbaglearning.com*
- *www.schoolofeverything.com*
- *www.fleet-tutors.co.uk*
- *www.bluetutors.co.uk*

More information on being a tutor:

- Free tutoring e-book - *www.thetutorpages.com/free-tutoring-ebook*
- Profitable Tutoring from A+ Tutors - *www.aplustutors.co.uk/tutors/profitable_tutoring-01.php*
- *www.tutorhub.org*

You Might Also Like

❑ Teacher
❑ Trainer
❑ Teaching Assistant

Other Business Ideas Beginning with 'T'

❑ Takeaways and restaurants franchisee
❑ Tie-dyeing and batik
❑ Tai Chi Teacher
❑ Translator

UNDER FIVES GROUP LEADER

What is it?

Under-fives groups are for pre-school children and are usually held in village halls or community centres. They help children play, learn, have fun and interact with others.

Tell me more...

Under-fives groups help children play, learn, have fun and interact with other children and include:

- Messy play
- Arts and crafts
- Music and dance/movement
- Speech and communication
- Cooking
- Baby yoga and massage
- Languages, including sign language

What are the benefits?

- You may be able to take your own children with you, although it will depend on the group and the age of your children. Caring for your own toddler while setting up and clearing away could be hard work.

- You can run as many or as few sessions as you want.

- You might be able to create your own franchise to sell to others.

- You could diversify e.g. you could also run children's parties or produce a CD.

- If you don't want to start from scratch, there are several franchises you could buy.

- If you have a background in childcare or education but fancy a change from school or nursery, this could be a rewarding new career.

Things to consider...

Parents may encourage you to charge on a per-session basis as it's more convenient for them. But you'll have costs to cover such as the hire of a hall, so you may need to charge on a term-by-term basis. You could make this more appealing by offering the first session for free or the first three sessions to be paid on a per-session basis.

Demand is likely to be term-time only, so will you need to budget for this or find other ways of earning an income for the other 12 weeks in the year? Or does term time working suit you?

Many Sure Start and children's centres have opened up over the last few years offering free pre-school sessions. You can compete with this, but you will need to think about what you have to offer that the Sure Start centres don't have. Alternatively, you could ask them if you could run sessions for them. If you can't beat them, join them!

When working out how much you could earn from running a pre-school group, don't forget to include the time you won't be paid directly for, e.g. setting up and clearing away, administration, lesson planning and preparation.

Check out the legal requirements, which will be different depending on the group you run. For example - do you need a Criminal Records Bureau check? What are the health and safety requirements? Do you need to be inspected by Ofsted? *The Pre-School Alliance Guide to Running Baby and Toddler Groups* (see the next page) is a good place to start.

If you're looking at buying a franchise, how long will it take you to earn back the franchise fee? What do you get with the franchise? Is this good value for money?

It may take you a couple of years to get a full group of children.

Further information

- The Pre-School Alliance - *www.pre-school.org.uk* - has a guide to running baby and toddler groups - www.pre-school.org.uk/parents/baby-and-toddler-groups

Franchises available include:

- *www.talking-tots.info*
- *www.musicalminis.co.uk*
- *www.artybobs.co.uk*
- and many more!

There are lots of mums who have set up their own groups without a franchise, check these out for some inspiration:

- *www.jellybeansmusic.com*
- *www.singasaurus.co.uk*
- *www.totsplay.co.uk*
- *www.messymob.co.uk*
- See the Family Friendly Working Business Opportunities Directory for more: *www.familyfriendlyworking.co.uk*

You might also like

- ❑ Children's party entertainer

VIRTUAL ASSISTANT

What is it?

A virtual assistant works remotely on tasks like administration, bookkeeping, event organisation, telephone answering and personal assistance.

Tell me more...

Small businesses who need admin support but don't want an employee can hire a VA for as many hours as they want. VAs usually work from their own home and many never meet their clients face-to-face.

What are the benefits?

- You can work flexible hours.
- You can choose the type of work you'd like to do.
- With technology such as call diverting, the internet and email, you can work from almost anywhere.

Things to consider...

Although this is a much more flexible way of working than being employed, you will still need to meet deadlines (usually for several different clients at the same time) and be available when your clients need you. This takes a high level of organisation and being realistic about the hours you can work.

Many people with administration and PA experience are great at their job, but are used to being 'behind the scenes people'. This means that getting out there and selling themselves doesn't come naturally to them. You can overcome this, but you will need to think about how you will do it.

The concept of virtual assistance is still new to many people so you may have to explain what you do and how you can be of benefit to them.

Having a niche is the key to building a business - don't try to do all types of administration for all types of business.

As a remote worker, potential clients will need to trust that you can get the work done to a high standard and on time. This means projecting a professional image at all times. If your home makes this difficult (if you have screaming children in the background when you answer the phone!), then you'll need to create some systems to get around this. For example, using a telephone answering service when the children are at home.

Further information

- *The Virtual Assistant Handbook* by Nadine Hill - *www.thedreampa.co.uk*

- The UK Association of Virtual Assistants - *www.ukava.co.uk*

- Society of Virtual Assistants - *www.societyofvirtualassistants.co.uk*

- International Association of Virtual Assistants - *www.iava.org.uk*

If you want to become a virtual assistant there are various courses on and offline to help you. Try:

- *www.vasuccessgroup.co.uk*
- *www.vact.co.uk*

WEBSITE OWNER
(INFORMATION)

What is it?

Earning an income online by providing information rather than by selling a physical product.

Tell me more...

Online shops are a popular choice for mums who want to run their own business. Alternatively, you could create a website that provides information. This might be:

- A listings website showing what's on in your local area.

- A blog. Blogs ('weblogs') are websites which started out as online diaries, but many have now developed into websites that provide information, news and opinion on a specific subject or to a particular community.

- A social network or membership site where members pay a monthly fee to receive information, training or coaching on a particular subject. This could be as a video, podcast, e-book or e-course.

- A website selling an information product such as e-books and e-courses.

You can earn money from an information site by:

- Selling advertising space, much like a magazine

- Google Adsense - Google will pay you when a visitor to your site clicks on an advertiser's link (there are other similar programmes too).

- Affiliate links - you are paid commission when visitors to your site buy from a site you are affiliated to.

- Selling an e-book, e-course or other information product on your website.

- Becoming an expert in your subject could lead to delivering courses, writing print books, coaching or being a consultant.

What are the benefits?

- You can work whenever and wherever you want
- It's cheap and easy to get started
- You can write about a subject that you love and get paid for it.

Things to consider...

It's very easy to start a blog which means there are millions of blogs out there. Getting large numbers of people to visit your site will take a lot of work, including online networking and writing lots of content plus some knowledge of search engine optimisation. You'll also need to write great content that will bring people back to your site again and again.

Getting people to spend money on your website will mean you need to convince them that what you have to sell is of value to them and that you're an expert in your area. This can take a lot of trial and error to discover what works for your audience, as well as giving away lots of information for free.

Further information

Examples of information websites run by mums:

- *www.businessplusbaby.com* and *www.familyfriendlyworking.co.uk* - blogs
- *www.parentpages.co.uk* – a website giving local information and things to do for parents
- *www.webmums.com* – a membership site

Want to try blogging?

- You can start your own blog for free at *www.wordpress.com* or *www.blogger.com*. To make money from blogging you'll need to move on from a free blog, but this is a good way to see if blogging is for you. Have a look at *www.littlemumpreneur.com* for a free course to help you get your blog started.

- To learn about making money from blogging see *www.problogger.net*. For advice on writing content check out *www.copyblogger.com*.

You might also like
- ❏ Web designer
- ❏ Web marketer

Other Business Ideas Beginning with 'W'
- ❏ Wholesaler
- ❏ Will writing
- ❏ Woodwork
- ❏ Writing

YOGA TEACHER OR PERSONAL TRAINER

What is it?

If you're a fitness fan and love sharing your enthusiasm with others, have you thought about turning your passion into a business?

Tell me more...

Running exercise classes of any sort can be a flexible career that you can build up to fit the hours you have available. If you want to work school hours you could offer classes for pre-schoolers, post pregnancy classes or specialise in exercise for older people. If you want to work evenings you could start by running a class one night a week and build up to offer further sessions as your popularity grows and you get more enquiries.

What are the benefits?

Working as a Yoga Teacher, Personal Trainer or Exercise Teacher allows you to do something you are interested in and help others at the same time as running a flexible and family friendly business.

Things to consider...

You need to be an enthusiastic participant in your preferred form of exercise for some years to be accepted on many training courses. Yoga'd Up, for example, require that you have been practising Yoga for 5 years.

You also need to be able to:

- analyse other peoples strengths, weaknesses and motivating factors
- nurture and develop people
- work with all sorts of different people
- motivate yourself and others
- live a healthy lifestyle

If you need to retrain, remember that not all training courses are run at family friendly times. You may find that you need to travel some distance or stay away for a number of weekends. Training can cost several thousand pounds. Many courses offer a combination of distance and face to face learning which will help you fit study round the family. And some courses allow you to build up your expertise so you can start your business and continue to develop your knowledge while taking further modules.

Depending on what you choose to train for, you could find yourself studying topics such as Anatomy and Physiology, Nutrition and Behaviour Change as well as exercise. If you can choose a course that allows you to develop a speciality this can help you show potential clients how you have unique skills and are different to other instructors or trainers. You may choose to specialise in working with certain groups or add in training in different disciplines.

You may choose to look for part time employment: if you plan to do this at ask local gyms about the sort of qualifications that they want before committing to a training course.

Building up classes or clients can take some time, and profits are not always high. You'll need good marketing skills both to get going and also to make the most of traditional times of year when people are looking to exercise more. You can have problems finding venues: suitable venues may be costly or fully booked. Once you have a good venue, though, it can help you attract clients.

Working one to one with people as a personal trainer means that you need find fewer clients, but your business is more dependent on those that you have. Whatever sort of fitness business you run, your earnings are limited to the time you have available and you will need to think about what you might do if you are ill or need to cover a family crisis. Expanding your business so that you are working with other teachers or trainers can take the pressure off – but also will mean that you have further administrative tasks to do.

Further information

General Fitness Training:

- National Register of Personal Trainers - *www.nrpt.co.uk* - a register of qualified and insured trainers. Offers a database of preferred training companies.

- Find recognised courses at The Register of Exercise Professionals - *http://reps.training.exerciseregister.org* - The Register of Exercise Professionals safeguards and promotes the health and interests of people who are using the services of exercise and fitness instructors, teachers and trainers. It uses a process of self-regulation that recognises industry-based qualifications, practical competency, and requires exercise professionals to work within a Code of Ethical Practice. Members of the Register are given a card and registration certificate to prove their qualification and membership. Also known as the Exercise Register it operates in the UK and across the world to recognise personal achievement and competencies of qualified exercise professionals.

- YMCAfit - *www.ymcafit.org.uk* - offer a wide variety of courses for people who would like to become a fitness instructor including personal trainer, gym instructor, exercise to music, and kids' fitness courses. YMCAfit qualifications are on the Register of Exercise Professionals and are recognised throughout the UK, Europe, New Zealand and Australia.

Pilates Teacher Training:

- *www.pilatesfoundation.com*

Yoga Teacher Training:

- British Wheel of Yoga - www.bwy.org.uk
- Yoga Alliance - *www.yogaalliance.com*

Training to teach Preschoolers, school children or pregnant women:

- Yoga Bugs - *www.yogabugs.com*
- Yoga Bananas - *www.yogabananas.com*
- Pregnancy yoga - *www.whyoga.com* or *www.birthlight.com*

You might also like

❑ Under 5s group leader

AT-A-GLANCE CHECKLIST OF GREAT BUSINESS IDEAS FOR MUMS

Costs assume that you own a computer.

Don't forget business insurance.

Some careers require retraining.

Startup cost will be significantly higher if you buy a franchise.

	CAN BE DONE ANY TIME	SOME FLEXIBILITY	FIXED HOURS	START UP COSTS < £500	START UP COSTS > £500	TRAINING NEEDED?
Antenatal Teacher		✓		✓		✓
Bookkeeper		✓		✓		✓
Children's Party Entertainer		✓		✓		
Drop Shipping	✓			✓		
Ebay	✓			✓		
Franchisee		✓			✓	
Graphic Designer		✓		✓		✓
Holistic Therapist		✓		✓		
Inventor	✓				✓	
Journalist		✓		✓		
Kitchen Cleaner		✓		✓		
Life Coach		✓		✓		✓
Magazine Owner	✓				✓	
Nail Technician		✓		✓		✓
Online Store Owner	✓			✓	✓	
Party Planner		✓		✓		
Tutor			✓	✓		✓
Under Fives Group Leader		✓		✓		
Virtual PA		✓		✓		
Website Owner	✓			✓		
Yoga Teacher or Personal Trainer		✓		✓		✓

ABOUT YOUR BUSINESS IDEA

BY NOW WE HOPE WE'VE SPARKED A BUSINESS IDEA OR TWO. THE NEXT STEP IS TO CHECK THAT IT'S GOING TO BE A SUCCESS FOR *YOU*. IT'S TEMPTING TO SKIP THIS STEP, BUT WE'D LIKE TO ENCOURAGE YOU TO KEEP GOING.

Why? Well, when you get some thoughts down on paper (or screen), the idea stops being a thought and becomes real. And once your business is real, you can ask yourself the important questions. Is it likely to earn you the income you want and deserve? Do you feel passionate enough about the business idea to pursue it?

Try to avoid getting get bogged down when you're filling in the gaps. It's much better to have a rough plan than to aim for a perfect one then end up with no plan at all. Plus, the thinking that you'll do as you fill in the gaps is as important as what you'll write.

My business will...

(What will it sell? What service will it provide?)

My Customers

My customers will be...

(Be specific, e.g. new mums in their 20s and 30s in
Northamptonshire)

My business will solve this problem for my customers...

(Again, be specific e.g. a private tutor may write 'getting children a
good grade in GCSE Maths')

I can check that customers want this product/service by...

(e.g. using an online forum, asking around people I know, starting a
blog and ask for comments, filling in questionnaires at my children's
school gates, using an online questionnaire such as
www.surveymonkey.com)

My customers will find me...

(e.g. on the web, by word of mouth, at a business networking group, on a post office notice board, in a community magazine advert...)

The Money

The money COMING IN to my business in the first year will be...

Take a look at the table on page 109. First, we are going to fill in the top section 'Money In'.

Estimate at how many items or hours of your time you are likely to sell in your first month. Then multiply this by your hourly rate or cost per item. This will give you how much money will be coming into your business in the first month from your sales. Repeat this for the rest of the months. (You can start with any month you like, of course). Providing you market your business effectively, you can usually expect the number of hours/items you can sell to increase as the months go by. This is because it takes time to get customers.

In the 'Other' row, enter any other money that will be coming into your business, say from loans or from your own personal money.

The money GOING OUT of my business in the first year will be...

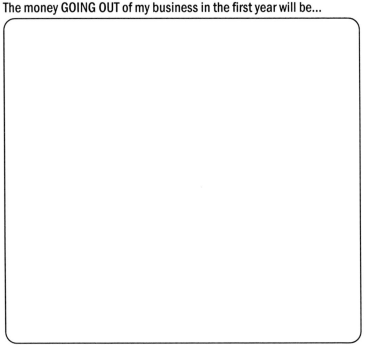

The bottom section of the table on page 109 covers your expenses. You may not have to pay all of these, especially in your first year. But we wanted to include all the expenses you are likely to have to pay so you don't have any nasty shocks later on!

Fill in the expenses you're likely to have to pay in the first year. Some will be very rough estimates. For example, there is no quick and easy way of estimating how much tax you will have to pay. Even a rough estimate is better than completely overlooking an expense.

Note that your own pay is a business expense. It's important that you include your own salary, rather than just taking what's left over when everyone else has been paid. Otherwise you risk not getting paid at all! Although you may decide not to pay yourself a salary for the first few months or year, you should have a planned date for when you will get paid. Work out how many hours you want to work a month and then multiply this by your hourly rate. Remember to pay yourself for all the time you spend on the business, including the hours you can't bill clients directly for (e.g. time spent marketing and doing admin).

Put the expenses you need to spend to get started in the 'Start Up Expenses' column and the ongoing expenses in the monthly columns. For example, you may need to pay to buy a piece of equipment before you get started, then set aside some money every month for repairs so you have some money put aside ready for a breakdown or maintenance.

You will need to pay back your start-up loan (and probably interest too). If you plan to borrow from a bank, put in the monthly amount you will have to pay back. If you are borrowing from a relative, divide the amount by the number of months you want to take to pay the money back, and enter that amount each month. If you are funding the business from your own savings, you should still aim to pay yourself back.

Add up your expenses for each column.

This is how I know that my business is profitable...

Now for the moment of truth!

Work out: Money In Minus Money Out...

If you your number is greater than zero, you have a profitable business. This may take a few months or even years. Can you cope in the meantime? Is this enough profit to allow you to develop your business, or do you need to look at your figures again?

If it's less than zero, you need to do some more work. Can you cut down your expenses without your business suffering? Are your prices too low? Is it going to take longer than you thought to break even?

If you want to wholesale in the future remember that you need to pitch your price so retail partners can make up to 50% profit. If you aren't VAT registered now, but may be in the future factor this in as otherwise your prices will face a sharp hike when your register – or your profits will fall.

My Competitors

My main competitors are...

(Do a Google search to find out)

My product/service is different from my competitors' because...

(e.g. my product is slightly different (how?), I'll be meeting
a very specific need that my competitors are not, I'll be
offering a better quality service...)

Me

I will work from...

(home, rented desk, office/factory, home plus rented storage space,
shop, be mobile)

I need this qualification/to take this course/to gain this experience before I launch my business...

These people can help or support me...

(e.g. accountant, business adviser, friend for moral support and childcare help, other business mums for moral support)

I'm starting this business because... (tick any that apply)

❑ *It's the only way I can find work that fits around my family*

❑ *I can't afford/find suitable childcare*

❑ *I want to be my own boss*

❑ *I've got a passion for this product/service*

❑ *I've spotted a gap in the market*

❑ *People tell me I'm great at this and that they would pay for me to do/make/sell it*

❑ *I'm ready for a new challenge and/or a fresh start*

❑ *I've had enough of the 9-to-5/being a stay at home mum*

❑ *Other... _____*

❑ *Other... _____*

❑ *Other... _____*

MONEY IN	STARTUP INCOME	Jan	Feb	Mar	Apr	May	Jun	Jul	Aug	Sep	Oct	Nov	Dec	TOTAL
Sales														
Other Income														
TOTAL £														
MONEY OUT	STARTUP EXPENSES													
Materials														
Stock														
Insurance														
Postage and stationery														
Buying and repairing equipment														
Travel														
Telephone														
Marketing/advertising														
Postal address/mail forwarding service/PO Box														
Website (creation and ongoing costs)														
Paying back start-up loan														
Loan interest														
My pay														
Tax														
National Insurance														
VAT														
Computer Expenses (hardware, software, broadband)														
Accountancy fees (and other professionals)														
Bank charges														
TOTAL £														
Money In minus Money out														

How do you feel about your business now?

Do you feel completely overwhelmed by the amount of work ahead? Are you concerned that you have so many unanswered questions? Don't worry, this is normal! Look beneath all these feelings and see if you have a spark of excitement or perhaps a sense of determination to make this work.

Ask yourself this question – "Do I want to go ahead and start this business?"

For this business to be a success, you must want to start it. If you begin it only because, for example:

- You feel you should
- You feel you have no other alternative
- It seems like a logical step to take
- Nobody else is doing it

The chances are you won't stick at it for very long.

By the way, it's fine to start a business because you want to and it seems like a logical step to take. You may have several motivating factors and that's fine as long as one of them is a real desire to start your own business. It's also fine for some of your motivating factors to be 'negative', for example you can't find the right childcare to enable you to do your job.

So, do you want to start this business?

If the answer is 'no'...

Is it because starting a business isn't right for you at the moment?

Maybe you have enough to deal with for the time being? There's nothing wrong with that at all. But put all your business notes in a safe place just in case you need them later. It's surprising how circumstances change – in a couple of years you may find you're itching to get your business started.

Do you want to start a business, just not THIS business?

This can be very frustrating, but don't let it get you down. Can you identify the problem with this business? If you can, then you know what to avoid when looking for your next business idea. It's probably best to get looking for your next business idea straight away so you don't lose your momentum.

Is it because you're lacking confidence? Feeling overwhelmed? Need more support?

What is missing? Be very specific.

If it's confidence, what exactly is stopping you? Do you believe you're not good enough? That people like you don't start businesses? Once you've pinned down the belief you can work on it. How can you prove to yourself that you're good enough? Can you find people just like you that are running businesses? You could also read books on building confidence or perhaps take a course.

If you need more support, what type of support do you need and where could you get it? Perhaps you need to talk to like-minded people or mums who are already running businesses? Do you need to get your childcare sorted out so you have space to think and enough free time? If you need business advice, information or training, try your local Chamber of Commerce or Enterprise Agency. And remember that you don't have to be an expert at everything to run a business: you can find other business mums who will help you with everything from admin to IT support to bookkeeping. Just join a networking group and you'll be amazed at how many people can help you get your business off the ground. There is a directory of networking groups for mums on *www.familyfriendlyworking.co.uk*.

If the answer is 'yes', and you're keen to go ahead then here are three more questions to ask yourself ...

Will this business give me the income I want and deserve?

When you're self employed, it's easy to work incredibly hard but still earn less than minimum wage. We believe that you should, and can, earn a decent income for your efforts; otherwise you'd be better off getting a job. At least you'd get paid holidays that way!

Looking carefully at the numbers at this early stage is vital to earning what you deserve. Remember that many businesses take months or years to become profitable, and plan for this. Look back at page 106. By your twelfth month in business, will your business be earning enough to cover your monthly expenses and more?

Before your business is fully profitable, it will need to bring in enough money to:

- Cover the monthly expenses
- Pay back a proportion of your start-up loan each month (you could spread the repayments over twelve months or twenty four months, for example)
- Pay tax and National Insurance
- Pay your salary

At this stage, most of your numbers will be estimates – and that's fine. Almost every new business owner has to make some guesses at the start. Even so you'll have a good idea of how many widgets or hours you need to sell every month, and at what price, to earn an income for yourself. Is this realistic?

If it's going to take more than twelve months for your business to earn you an income, can you survive in the meantime?

Do I have the time, energy, investment required to run this business?

And if you don't have these now, how can you get them? Start noting down small steps to get you closer to where you need to be to start the business.

Can I be available at the right times to keep my clients happy?

In the 'All about you' section you will have mapped out the hours in the week you have to work on your business. Are these going to be right for your clients? If your main working hours are evenings and weekends, will your clients expect you to be available nine-to-five on weekdays?

If this is a problem for you, here are some solutions. If your clients are mostly other mums, they may be sympathetic if your toddler talks in the background when they phone you. You could partner up with another mum who works the 'opposite' hours to you, like a job share. You could use a telephone answering service to cover the hours that your children are in the house and then call back later. Or you could manage your clients' expectations so that they deal with you mostly by email and over the web – depending on your clients, of course.

Although you won't want to be on call twenty-four hours a day, technology can help you give a full-time service even though you may work part-time hours. You can answer emails on your Blackberry while keeping an eye on your children in the park, for example. Telephone answering services are now affordable even if you're a one-woman businesses. You can use voicemail and 'out of office' emails to tell customers when you're next available and what to do if there's an emergency.

Here are those four questions again

❑ Do I want to start this business?

❑ Will this business give me the income I want and deserve?

❑ Do I have the time, energy, investment required to run this business?

❑ Can I be available at the right times to keep my clients happy?

If you can answer 'yes' to these four questions, congratulations! You have a business idea that has a great chance of success!

Next steps

So what are your next steps? Here are our suggestions.

❑   Go back to over the questions starting on page 101. Try to expand your responses so you get a more detailed plan for your business. Where are the gaps? What else do you need to know? Who do you need to speak to?

❑   Get yourself some business knowledge – you can read books and websites or take a short course (don't worry, there's no need to get a university qualification!)

❑   Do some market research. It's easy to get so fired up by your business idea that you forget to ask if anyone actually wants what you are selling! But time invested in market research now will save a lot of wasted effort and money later on.

❑   Investigate sources of funding.

❑   Make a prototype of the product or test out the service. Ask people for feedback.

Action steps

Over to you! The next steps I need to take to get my business started are:

USEFUL RESOURCES

Books

- *Family Friendly Working* by Antonia Chitty
- *Believing You Can Do It, Emotional Confidence* and more books on developing confidence, self esteem and assertiveness by Gael Lindenfield
- *Kitchen Table Tycoon* by Anita Naik
- *Make It Your Business* by Lucy Martin & Bella Mehta
- *Millionaire Mumpreneur* by Mel McGee
- *Mum Ultrapreneur* by Susan Odev & Mark Weeks
- *Secrets of Successful Women Entrepreneurs* by Sue Stockdale
- *Supermummy: The Ultimate Mumpreneur's Guide to Online Business Success* by Mel McGee
- *The Mumpreneur Guide's Start Your Own Business Book* by Antonia Chitty
- *The Virtual Assistant Handbook* by Nadine Hill

Websites

- Business Link - *www.businesslink.gov.uk*
- Business Plus Baby - *www.businessplusbaby.com*
- Enterprise Nation - *www.enterprisenation.com*
- Everywoman - *www.everywoman.com*
- Family Friendly Working - *www.familyfriendlyworking.co.uk*
- Giant Potential - *www.giantpotential.ning.com*
- Mums Club - *www.mumsclub.co.uk*
- Mums The Blog - *www.mumstheblog.co.uk*
- Start Up Donut - *www.startupdonut.co.uk*
- The Mumpreneur Guide - *www.themumpreneurguide.co.uk/secretblog*

TIME TO COMMIT

Thank you for reading this book. We hope that if you were stuck before, now you have an idea of how to progress your dream of a flexible balance between fulfilling work and time with the family.

If you have decided what business you would like to pursue, write down the next steps that you need to take to start turning the idea into reality. Write down what you need to do and when you will aim to do it: making this commitment right now will make it much more likely that you will succeed.

I will...

by _____ (insert date)

I will...

by _____ (insert date)

I will...

by _____ (insert date)

If you are still unsure about the right business idea for you, take time to do more research. Write down three ideas that appeal and commit to look into each of them.

I will find out more about...

I will find out more about...

by _____ (insert date)

I will find out more about...

by _____ (insert date)

Make this commitment and you are taking the first steps on the road to a better life for you and your family.

Antonia Chitty
Family Friendly Working
www.familyfriendlyworking.co.uk

Helen Lindop
Business Plus Baby
www.businessplusbaby.com

Lightning Source UK Ltd.
Milton Keynes UK
18 September 2010

160017UK00001B/8/P